C000143513

CELTIC CORNWALL

By the same author

Dictionary of Country Furniture
A Woman's Place
Cottage Industries

CELTIC CORNWALL

MARJORIE FILBEE

CONSTABLE · LONDON

First published in Great Britain 1996
by Constable and Company Ltd
3 The Lanchesters, 162 Fulham Palace Road
London W6 9ER
Copyright © 1996 Marjorie Filbee
ISBN 0 09 476 090
Set in Monophoto Garamond 12pt by
Servis Filmsetting Ltd, Manchester
Printed in Great Britain by
St Edmundsbury Press Ltd
Bury St Edmunds, Suffolk

A CIP catalogue record for this book
is available from the British Library

To my great-grandson, Benjamin Jack Green

Contents

Illustrations

Acknowledgements

The help I have received from the authors, ancient and modern, of the books listed in the bibliography at the end of this book is inestimable. I acknowledge the great debt I owe them and am very conscious of the extensive knowledge and learning they have contributed by their writing to the history of Cornwall, a very small part of which I have been able to put into my book.

I am especially grateful to David Johnston for his help and advice on the earlier chapters, and to Charles Thomas and the many archaeologists who have contributed to the journals of the Cornwall Archaeological Society. My special thanks go to Roger Penhallurick of Truro Museum, to Tony Bayfield of the Cornwall Archaeological Unit, to Joyce Greenham, Andrew Langdon and Richard Filbee for their help in finding and supplying photographs. My thanks to the Tate at St. Ives for the photograph of the Barbara Hepworth sculpture and to Sir Alan Bowness, the Hepworth Estate for permission to reproduce it; to Peter Prideaux-Brune for permission to reproduce the photograph of Sir Bevil Grenville, and to the National Trust for the photographs on pages 58, 88, 93, 97, 98, 113, 138; to the Trust and A.F. Kersting for the photograph of Richard Carew of Antony; and to the Hand Bench of Exeter for illustrations. My very grateful thanks go to Felicity Wooldridge for typing the manuscript.

Introduction

TODAY it is not difficult to imagine the landscape of Cornwall as it lay in wait for the Celtic dawn to rise over it. This was long before the Celts actually put in an appearance in the fourth and fifth centuries BC.

There is a timelessness about the county which makes it possible to look backwards for thousands of years without difficulty – so much has changed so little.

It was all there from the beginning. The rocks and stones that would provide them with work, wealth and homes. The hills and moors that would give them pasture for their flocks. The leafy valleys, rivers and streams that would provide the setting where they could find the spirits they worshipped. All around them they would find the sea, sometimes calm, sometimes terrifyingly stormy, but over which they had never been afraid to travel, it was so in keeping with their own characters.

This was the ideal setting for a people who were to influence Cornwall for many centuries to come, down to today, when so much Celtic culture is still in evidence. If we look forward from these early times, there has never been a century when the characteristics and strengths of the Celts were not brought to the fore in the Cornish people by the events of each particular age.

They were not the first people to be attracted to Cornwall, or the last. Earlier visitors had wandered the county ten thousand years ago. Hunting and gathering their food as they moved from place to place, they left their flint tools as they went as evidence of their presence, mainly along the coastal areas and high moors of the county. Eventually these itinerant people settled down about six thousands years ago as farmers, fishermen and, at a surprisingly early date, as miners, owing to the rich mineral wealth on which Cornwall stands. This at a time when the rest of Britain was still mainly occupied with agriculture.

They found tin washed down from the granite hills lying as black pebbles in the gravel of the many streams. From early days they traded

The hillfort at Carn Brea, Illogan

it with countries far afield. This gave them many early contacts with the outside world, the sea as always their main highway.

They began to influence changes in the landscape, clearing forests to grow crops, selecting those plants and trees that would provide their food. They were primarily farmers, living in groups on the uplands of the county, domesticating the animals that would become so important to them.

Cornwall has the oldest village in Britain at the hilltop site of Carn Brea, south-west of Redruth in west Cornwall. It was a Stone Age settlement, two acres in extent, defended by a massive stone wall.

Some of the stones used to build the wall weighed in excess of two to three tons – no mean feat of construction for Cornish man in Neolithic times. Some had to be lifted over one metre from the ground into position. Hundreds of arrowheads found inside the defensive wall lead to the conclusion that the summit of Carn Brea was not always a peaceful place. Possibly defences were needed for protection, not only from invaders, but from competition from other tribes as the population increased.

Within this wall archaeologists found traces of wooden buildings of six thousands years ago. Outside, areas had been cleared for growing crops, although corn-growing was difficult in the hard soil and pasture for grazing more important. As the land was cleared of stones, these were used for building homes, walls and hedges. So much survives in Cornwall because the granite rocks are indestructible, although bones, iron and pottery cannot survive for long in the acid soil. The whole area was surrounded by defensive ramparts, with fifteen stone-lined entrances. It was probably one of several hilltop centres at this early date for the distribution and exchange of goods and the importing of objects and raw materials by land and sea from a wide variety of sources. The polished stone axes they produced at Carn Brea have been found all over Britain, particularly the greenstone axes unique to Cornwall. The greenstone was found at St Ives, Marazion, Camborne and the Penwith peninsula. It produced an axe less liable to fracture than those made of other stone. Cornwall also produced axe-hammers and battle-axes for trade with Wessex as early as 2500 BC. Pottery cups and wide-mouthed bowls and jars were exported to other areas of the south coast between 3000 and 2700 BC.

The jars had rounded bases, sometimes with lugs by which they could be lifted, perforated so that a thong could be inserted, for carry-ing or suspending over a fire. Some of these bowls with trumpet-shaped lugs are peculiar to this south-western area of Britain, but are also found in Brittany, an area with which Cornwall had connections from the ear-liest days. Being fragile, the pottery was most likely to have travelled by sea, as much of it has been found unbroken at various sites along the south coast of England.

The castle that can be seen today at Carn Brea is of medieval origin, but Celtic as well as Roman coins have been found there, testifying to occupation in Iron Age times when the hill was refortified. Many Cornish farms stand today on the sites of prehistoric farms, as churches now stand where early man once worshipped. It seems that the Cornish have always appreciated a good site, whatever purpose it originally served, and needed a strong reason for usage to be changed. Some of these ancient hillforts were again in use in the Civil War of the seven-teenth century. Carn Brea was still at the centre of activity when tin

Remains of neolithic tomb, Lanyon Quoit, in 1858

mining was at the height of production in the area in the eighteenth century.

It is the now peaceful and silent grassy mounds, humps and ramparts of Cornwall which tell us the most about how and where prehistoric people lived and died. Our knowledge of many of the objects they made and used comes from those found in the communal burial chambers of the period. These massive stone chambers or quoits were originally covered with large amounts of earth. Now they stand stark against the skyline of Bodmin Moor, or on the coastal areas of the peninsula. They were used for the burial of the dead over many years, their contents cleared out or moved aside from time to time to make way for new burials.

Many of the remains of these quoits have been altered or reconstructed in the last century. The best surviving examples are Pawton Quoit in north Cornwall, Trethevy Quoit north of Liskeard, Lanyon Quoit Madron and Zennor Quoit in the Penwith peninsula.

It is in Penwith that are found the entrance graves peculiar to this remote area, where an entrance passage is situated at the edge of a round burial mound.

By 2500 BC there is evidence of people from northern Europe in Cornwall. They came to be known as the Beaker people, from the pottery beakers they brought with them, along with a knowledge of bronze and metalworking and battle-axes. They found in Cornwall quantities of the components needed for the manufacture of bronze, copper and tin. They buried their dead not in communal chambers but in round mounds, each containing a single burial. Their beakers were decorated with impressive patterns on thin red ware, possible because of their skilful firing of the clay at a high temperature, skills obtained from their knowledge of smelting techniques. These were buried with them, together with some of their treasured possessions, tools and weapons, to provide for Beaker Man's journey to a life after death. His prayers were most likely to have been to the Earth Mother, the goddess of fertility, for his greatest need was probably men and animals and the food with which to feed them. That his prayers were answered can be seen by the large numbers of striking stone circles and menhirs, enormous standing stones some three to four and half metres high which he had sufficient manpower to erect. Menhir is a Celtic word for 'long stone'. Cornwall has such a wealth of these stones than they must have had great importance to early man. Many of them were brought long distances to the sites where they now stand. They testify to a compelling belief in something beyond the lives of the builders themselves, for them to make the great effort they did in the planning and construction of these monuments. Some they sited near important ancient trackways

Handled beaker from Gulval. 1600 BC. Height 6.3 inches

The Hurlers at Minions. Late 18th century drawing of bronze age stone circle

and trading routes; some were connected with burials. Bones and a beaker with a handle were buried at the base of a menhir at Try, near Gulval, in a small cist. Others were near menhirs at Trevennack, Paul, Trelew, Penrhyn and Sancreed.

Cornwall has the greatest variety of stone circles and nationally designated protected monuments of any region of comparative size in the British Isles. The Hurlers on Bodmin Moor is a good example and one of the most striking. A group of three circles aligned north-north-east to south-south-west, it is dated around 2000 BC. The two outside circles are round; the central circle is egg-shaped and composed of stones that have been worked, as had some of the stones at Stonehenge. As well as ceremonial or religious purposes, it is thought the stone circles may have had astronomical uses, to help the farming communities in planting and planning their crops, so important for their survival.

Later generations, not needing the stones for this reason, attached various legends to them. The Hurlers were thought to be members of a group of men playing the popular Cornish game of hurling, forbidden on the Sabbath, who were punished by being turned to stone. There is probably not one of the ancient stones of Cornwall that hasn't a legend attached to it now. Many were thought to have curative powers, a belief still strong in modern times. Others were thought to have been erected by giants – it was difficult to believe that primitive man could have performed such feats of strength. Even the rocks in the sea at Bedruthan Steps near Newquay were thought to be stepping stones for the giant Bedruthan.

Perhaps connected with the stone circles were several upright stones with large circular holes in them, whose use and purpose are unknown. The stone at Mên-an-Tol in West Penwith is round with a hole fifty-one centimetres in diameter. When children were passed through the hole three times it was said to cure them of the disease scrofula.

The hole in a stone in the garden of a cottage at Tolvan, Gweek, near the Helford River, is forty-four centimetres in diameter, but can only be viewed with permission.

There were also what were thought to be ceremonial sites at Castilly, at Lanivet near Bodmin, Castlewich in Caradon, and the Stripple Stones near Blisland. These were circular or oval featureless areas, sometimes with a stone or timber circle, a ditch and a bank. They were known as henge monuments, but had no defensive use. They may have been in use before the stone circles.

The remains of early settlements of these people have been found, usually on the uplands and coastal areas. Here they built circular stone houses, careful to put the entrances on the side that sheltered them from the prevailing winds, as they blew, then as now, from the Atlantic

Mên-an-Tol holed stone at Morvah

coast. Their walls were originally about one metre high, with roofs of thatch supported by a central post.

One such settlement, now buried under a housing estate at Trethellan near Newquay, was occupied for about three hundred years, from the fifteenth to the thirteenth centuries BC. Before the site was developed archaeologists were able to excavate it in 1987. They had time to obtain a large amount of information as to how the inhabitants lived so long ago. Today they are used to having to work against time as other sites are developed, before the evidence is lost forever.

Some of the seven round houses excavated appeared to be residential. There were also what were described as 'ritual' hollows whose use may never be known, but which add to the mystery surrounding so much that these people left behind. There were also wooden buildings in different styles which could have had various uses.

There were traces of the Beaker People having been there before them, and of iron age people using the site as a burial ground long after they left. A medieval farm, Trethellan Farm, gave its name to the area in the thirteenth century AD.

Each of the houses had been built over a hollow, some with walls constructed with a single ring of posts, some with a double. Each had a central hearth. Both slate and stone had been used for the hearths and

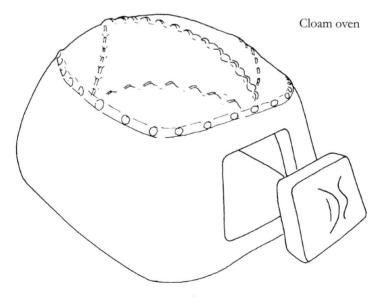

Cloam oven

for some of the entrances. Slate had also been used to make a slate box which functioned much in the way of the 'Dutch oven' that stood in front of a fire in an eighteenth century home to radiate heat to cook the food inside. There were the remains of what could have been a cloam oven. This was a popular means of cooking in a clay oven, many of which stood at the side of Cornish fireplaces until the present century. It was heated with burning furze, wood or peat. This was raked out when the food to be cooked was put in and the clay door closed. There are many signs that the cooking and preparation of food were a major occupation of the home in Bronze Age times, as they are today.

There were granite saddle querns and rubbing stones for grinding the grain that came from the oats, barley and beans growing in the fields nearby. There were whetstones used for sharpening tools and perhaps for smoothing animal skins for clothing. There were clay spindle shorls as evidence of textile activities, together with signs of a loom. There were two hammerstones which could have been used for mining but which might have had many other uses.

There was pottery of all sizes, mostly large tall pots with a variety of geometric designs, made by impressing a cord or fingers on the clay or incising with a tool. The clay came from the Lizard peninsula, either imported raw or as finished pots.

The acid soil of Cornwall, so good for rhododendrons, was not good for the preservation of animal bones, and there were only small remains of the bones of cattle, sheep, goat, pig and red deer.

The fields around the settlement also grew flax, which in prehistoric times may have been of more use for oil from its seeds than for textiles.

It is possible that the site was originally further from the sea than it is today and that there was oak and hazelwood for building. The latter could have provided the material for wattle fencing and fire screens, evidence of which was found inside the houses. Rushes and straw provided the thatched roofs and coverings for the floors.

There have been many changes in the coastline of Cornwall over the centuries. The sea rose in some places to cover settlement sites and forests, while in other places estuaries were silted up and sand dunes covered homes and churches.

A few bronze artifacts were found, including spearheads, a bronze

Gold lunula from a farm at St. Juliot

knife and bronze wire bracelets. By the later years of the Bronze Age metalworking was proceeding apace, with an increase in the varieties of tools used, together with ever-growing trade with Europe and Ireland. It is from Ireland that gold ornaments and bracelets were imported, possibly at first by a small élite group who needed to show their status in the community. These included gold lunulae, collars of thin gold sheet with incised patterns, similar to those also found in Brittany. Goldsmiths were now working on both sides of the Channel. Four gold lunulae found in Cornwall are made of Cornish gold but are of Irish design.

The most impressive gold object discovered in a barrow on Bodmin Moor at Rillaton, not far from the Hurlers stone circles, was a gold cup, similar to gold corrugated cups found in the royal tombs at Mycenae, Greece. This cup is now in the British Museum. It was lost for some years, but rediscovered in the dressing room of a later king, George V. Later goods found in graves in Cornwall included segmented blue

Gold cup from Rillaton, Linkinhorne, c. 1500 BC. 3¼ inches high

faience beads, manufactured in the eastern Mediterranean, and also found in the royal tombs at Mycenae. The Cornish trading links were now extending far and wide.

Around 1000 BC the Bronze Age people of Cornwall began the building of hillforts. By the seventh century BC iron was gradually replacing bronze, and with the arrival of the Celts, hillforts and iron-working were to become permanent features of Cornish life.

The site at Trethellan Farm left one or two unsolved mysteries, which may have influenced the next visitors there a thousand years later. Perhaps to them these would not have been mysteries at all. These people were nearer to the thoughts and beliefs of the former inhabitants than are we. At least we can understand that the hearths of these homes were at the heart of them. But underneath the hearth in one house, while it was inhabited, the body of a young man had been formally and carefully buried. The hearth had continued to be used after this event, which took place at a time when the usual method of burial was by cremation, with the ashes placed in a pottery urn that would then have been interred. This adds to a mystery that may never be solved. Not far from the house that featured this burial was what has been described as a 'ritual' structure, for want of more knowledge. This was not a hollow, but a unique small square stone building, with four drystone walls and a levelled floor that showed no sign of wear.

When the Bronze Age site was eventually abandoned, the area was left vacant for nine hundred years. The next visitors were the Iron Age

Celts, who do not appear to have inhabited the site or built houses on it. For reasons that are not apparent, they used the site as a formal cemetery, with twenty-one graves, unlined and unmarked, some containing single burials, some double, and some that could indicate that children had been buried with adults, perhaps as a family.

There were no rich finds in these graves, although there were bronze and iron brooches which had probably fastened the clothes in which the bodies were buried.

What had induced these people to make their burial ground here? It would not be impossible for Celtic minds to have sensed something special about such an ancient site. Perhaps the stories, oral tradition and legends that were to become such a feature of Celtic Cornish history told them more about the body under the hearth and the small stone building that we can ever know.

Cremation urn from St. Just. 20¼ inches high.

CHAPTER 1

The Arrival of the Celts

THE CELTIC DAWN rose gradually in Cornwall. It was almost as if it drifted in with the mists that so often surround the Cornish coasts, perhaps arriving first as ideas, influencing the Bronze Age inhabitants, almost unnoticed. There was no blinding flash, no great battle or memorable invasion. Small groups arrived from north-western Europe, where they had been established over the previous two hundred years, reaching Cornwall in the sixth to fourth centuries BC. Some may have entered the county from Ireland, with whose people Cornwall had long been in contact. A Greek writer in the sixth century BC wrote that Brittany traded with both Albion and Ierne, Greek versions of Irish Celtic names for Britain and Ireland.

Iron was soon to replace bronze for implements for both farming and building, making both easier and more efficient. Iron ploughs could cultivate fertile valleys. Iron scythes could cut more grass for hay. Improved farm buildings for cattle enabled better animals to be bred. To what extent this ironware was used for fighting can only be imagined from the numbers of hillforts and fortified farmsteads that appeared throughout south western Britain by the fourth century BC. Many had originated in the previous Bronze Age, but were now reoccupied and given more elaborate defences. The single rampart that had been the usual Bronze Age defence became forts with multiple defences. In some cases the ramparts of earth had wooden palisades on top. In Cornwall it was possible for many of the defences to be entirely of stone.

Chûn Castle hillfort on the Land's End peninsula had two massive stone ramparts, originally about six metres high, but now greatly reduced as the stones were taken away to provide buildings in Penzance. There was a stone-lined well within the fort and traces of buildings of the sixth century AD against the inner wall, built over earlier Iron Age round houses. The remains of an elaborate smelting furnace for tin has been found in the fort. These hillforts were probably trading centres, as they had been in Bronze Age times.

Near the fort is Chûn Quoit, a neolithic chamber tomb. This had four large stone slabs with a massive capstone 3.4 metres by 3.1 metres. The remains of the circular mound that originally covered it can still be seen.

The Cornish Celts were a tribal people, so no doubt there was much competition between them for land and special vantage points. They were part of the tribe of the Dumnonii, whose members were also found in Ireland, Devon and Somerset. They were skilled craftsmen, metalworkers and builders, but first and foremost a pastoral people living in close harmony with the land. They spoke a language that had probably been long understood by Bronze Age people. It has left its mark on the English language, and is still spoken in various forms in Scotland, Ireland, Wales and Cornwall. Cornish and Breton, the language of Brittany, were very similar in the Middle Ages.

There had always been very close Cornish connections with northern France, when in early days this Atlantic peninsula was known as Armorica (the land by the sea). Many of the Cornish settled there during the fifth and sixth centuries AD, when 'Armorica' became 'Brittany'; a clear indication of extensive immigration from south-west Britain.

The interiors of the Cornish hillforts show a considerable degree of planning, with large round houses as well as rectangular storage units. However, more widespread in Cornwall than the hillforts were the 'rounds', enclosures with widely spaced ramparts, situated on the slopes of hills or on flat ground. These had houses that were often next to the ramparts, leaving the centre clear for the farming activities of the inhabitants. These rounds, it seems, were not for defence or tribal-built, but safe areas for the needs of small family communities of independent pastoral farmers, to protect their livestock, for this was one of the Celts' greatest sources of wealth. Some of these rounds were in use until around AD 600. There were small rectangular fields near many of these rounds, probably for growing crops. Rotary querns were in use and were employed along with the earlier saddle querns throughout the Iron Age period for grinding oats and barley.

Walkers along the beautiful coast of Cornwall will today come across the grassy ramparts of the cliff castles of the Iron Age. These are protected now not by warring tribesmen, but by the National Trust. The banks and ditches constructed across the necks of headlands turn them into enclosures similar to the rounds, protecting the inhabitants of the homes inside from intruders. The sea and cliffs sheltered them from any danger from the sea. Similar cliff castles are also found on the coastline of northern France. The earliest known cliff castle is Maen Castle at Sennen, Land's End, built in about the fourth century BC. It has a massive stone wall 3.7 metres thick, with an entrance facing east. There are post-holes indicating that there were once timber gates at the entrance. Whilst no remains of buildings were found inside the fort, the farmers who worked the fields outside must have lived not too far away, perhaps in a more sheltered spot.

The round houses inside many of the cliff castles were similar to those built by the Beaker People in the previous Bronze Age. Decorated pottery and many spindle whorls – pierced discs of stone, clay, slate or bone used to add weight at the end of a wooden spindle shaft to twist a thread from loose wool – were found. The remains of what could have been upright looms were also discovered.

At the cliff castle, the Rumps, at Polzeath, were the remains of three lines of defence, also with elaborate wooden gateways at the entrances,

Aerial view of Rumps Cliff Castle

and walkways over the top like a medieval castle. It was occupied from the fourth century BC to the first century AD. The pottery here was made of clay from the St Keverne area of the Lizard peninsula, clay that had been used since the Bronze Age. This pottery was so valued that it has been mended with rivets when broken.

Pottery found on ancient sites is often the chief means whereby archaeologists can date a site, and the earliest pottery found in the cliff castles is from the third century BC. The undecorated jars and bowls were thought to be copies of Bronze Age vessels. Later pottery had incised geometric and the curvilinear patterns that became so associated with the Celts. Analysis of pottery has become so scientific today that it is possible to tell not only where the production centres were, but also where the clay came from. This Iron Age pottery contained minerals from the gabbroic rocks of the Lizard. It was produced either by groups of potters resident here, or exported as clay for use in other areas. It was distributed through the ever-increasing networking of trading routes as the age progressed.

In the last century BC a different style of pottery is found, decorated with cordons, incised or added, alongside the earlier pottery. Similar cordoned pottery was imported from France to Dorset and Devon. The Cornish variety fashioned from the Lizard clay may be a copy of this, made with knowledge acquired from constant trade along the south coast. It was still being made in the fourth century AD.

The hillforts show that whoever lived there had considerable available manpower under their control to build them. Under the Celts, Cornwall became even more tribal-oriented, under strong leaders, than under the warriors of the Bronze Age. While it was the most westerly part of the region of Dumnonia, the Celtic name for the county was Cernyw (Kernow). In later Roman times it became known as Cornovia, 'a place of promontory-dwellers'. When the later Saxon word for strangers (*wealas*) was added to the Celtic, it became Cornwall.

Roman writers give us the first written evidence of the Celtic-speaking people in Cornwall. They were well thought of by these writers as hospitable and civilised people, by reason of their many contacts with foreign merchants.

The Roman occupation of the West Country extended in the main only as far as Exeter, where the town Isca, the administrative centre for the whole peninsula, was founded. In fact, the Romans did not make much impression at all on Cornwall, although it was incorporated into the administration at Exeter. The Celtic way of life continued throughout the period. While some items of Roman presence have been found – pottery and brooches, milestones for a planned Roman road which has not survived and the remains of a Roman fort at Nanstallon, near Bodmin – locally made pottery continued to be made and the people appear to have lived peacefully in the manner they had always known.

This may, of course, have been due to the distance of Cornwall from the rest of Roman activity in Britain. Maybe it was due to the Roman practice of leaving trusted local chiefs in occupation wherever possible. Many of the earlier hillforts were abandoned in the Roman period. Those that were still occupied reveal that the occupants had access to typical Roman ware, glass and metalwork.

Towards the end of the Roman occupation it seems that the Romans were becoming more interested in Cornwall, because of Cornish tin. Other supplies of tin in the empire were declining. Many ingots of Cornish tin of the second century AD have been found. It was used mainly in the manufacture of pewterware. The fort the Romans were building at Nanstallon, Bodmin was near a route from the Camel estuary to Fowey, a well-known and well-used trade route for centuries. The Romans must have had plans for its use before they had to abandon the country.

Celtic art in Cornwall is first found in the brooches and mirrors excavated from burials of the last century BC, decorated with the curves, scrolls and fantastic forms that were to be found later on the Celtic crosses of the Cornish Christian period, artforms that were later to inspire the wonderful illuminated manuscripts of the monks of the early Celtic Church.

Cornwall is one of the few areas of the Iron Age to have produced cemeteries, where many of these decorated metal artifacts have been found, such as those at Harlyn Bay and Trevone, near Padstow, as well as the cemetery at Trethellan Farm, Newquay. Many of the possessions were in burial mounds and the graves of women, who were of some importance in the Celtic world.

At Harlyn the cemetery contained 130 graves, stone-lined cists covered with slate slabs. In each grave was a crouched body with the head pointing to the north, unlike the bodies in similar Iron Age cemeteries in Brittany which contained extended inhumations. At Harlyn the inhabitants had used the local material in an unusual polished-slate industry making needles, awls and borers for leatherworking, and in this seaside place probably for the repairing and making of nets. As well as loomweights and spindle whorls for cloth-making, there were also quantities of shells found here, from which they could have made dyes to colour their cloth. Not surprisingly there was plenty of evidence that limpets and mussels formed a large part of their diet.

The round houses of Cornwall continued in use for many centuries, as late as the ninth century AD. In West Penwith are the remains of what are known as courtyard houses, a form of dwelling unique to this far western area of the county, the remains of those at Chysauster, Gulval, on the granite uplands of Land's End, being the best known and available for the public to see. Here there was a small village of nine courtyard houses either side of a central street. Each had several rooms

Aerial view of Chysauster courtyard village

incorporated into a single unit around an open courtyard, eight to ten metres across, the outer wall being anything up to 4.5 metres thick. The long paved entrance faced north-east, sheltering the houses from the prevailing south-westerly winds. The main living room of each house was opposite the entrance and had a stone hearth and a central stone with a socket to hold the main roof support. The buildings around the courtyard would have had thatched or turf roofs and, as well as the main room, included another long room, perhaps a workshop or stable.

The plan was certainly not Roman, although executed during the Roman occupation of Britain, but perhaps the Roman idea of separate rooms for different purposes was beginning to influence the builders at this time. A small garden or paddock was attached to each house with terraced fields beyond and a sunken road leading down to a stream for watering stock. Surface water was drained from the courtyard in slab-covered channels, which also brought water to the village. The pottery found on the site was locally made, but there were a few copies of some Roman types. This small farming community lived here in the second and third centuries AD, after which the site was peacefully abandoned. Thirty or forty of these courtyard houses are found over this area of Cornwall. They may have been particularly adapted to cope with the windswept conditions of Land's End.

A short distance from some of these houses is an underground chamber, consisting of a sloping trench about 1.5 metres wide and two metres deep lined with drystone walling and with a roof constructed of flat slabs. Such chambers are known as souterrains or fogous and, while it is possible they may have had religious uses or been refuges in times of danger, it is thought more likely that they were communal cellars for the storage of food, particularly as similar structures known as 'hulls' were in use in Cornwall in the present century. Like the fogous, today they are mostly found in the granite uplands of west Cornwall, near farmhouses and cottages. Hull is a Cornish word for a storage tunnel or cave. Fogou comes from the Cornish word 'fogo' for a cave. These were in use until recent times for the storage of farm and dairy produce before the advent of refrigerators, for they maintained a constant temperature in winter and summer.

Souterrains are also found in Brittany, but of a different construction. The Breton ones are tunnelled into the ground, not built in an open trench. The fogou at Carn Euny, Sancreed, is connected to a round house at the settlement there, which had been in existence from Bronze Age times. Stone houses had replaced earlier wooden ones. The main gallery of the fogou is twenty metres long. The settlement and the fogou had developed over a long period, before being peacefully abandoned in AD 400. Several of these fogous had underfloor drainage.

While fogous are found in rounds and courtyard houses, they are not evident in cliff castles. Probably the wind around the coasts was enough to keep both food and inhabitants fresh and well preserved.

Intriguing remains from the Roman period are those of the only Roman villa in Cornwall, found at Magor, in a river valley two miles north of Camborne, about one mile from the sea. It was excavated in 1931 and then covered up again for its protection. It is tempting to see this small bungalow-type dwelling as the first retirement or holiday home to be built in Cornwall – that is if we can be really sure that anyone ever retired or took a holiday in Roman Britain. It is possible that the owner was a Cornishman who had served in the Roman army or civil service further east in England, dreaming that one day he would return to Cornwall to end his days as many have done since. He built himself a home in the style to which he had become accustomed while living in a more populated area. This he did in the late second century AD, employing local craftsmen, Celtic workmen who were sufficiently competent to build a substantial stone building, but not quite up to carrying out the finer points of Roman architecture. They were more used to round houses – Roman right angles were foreign to them. The villa had none of the amenities, such as underfloor heating or a bath area, usual in villas further east. They did, however, build a corridor-type villa with six or seven rectangular rooms, having plastered walls with painted floral decorations. Two of the rooms had fireplaces, and there was a plain tessellated corridor running the length of the villa. It must have been a pleasant enough home for its owner, living there in comparative splendid isolation, although there was a round not too far away, and some farming activity nearby. In the later years of the Roman occupation, new homes were already being built in rounds, which were of oval shape, enabling the interiors to be free of supports and giving a larger living area. At Trethungy Round near St Austell there was a hearth and cooking pit, which may have had pots embedded in hot ashes below floor level, where the food could cook slowly as the fire died down.

The larger oval houses showed signs of having fitted wooden furniture. Increasing quantities of imported Roman pottery were found on sites of third and fourth century date, but Cornish ware continued to be made throughout the Roman period.

While much can be learnt about where the Celts lived in Cornwall in the early centuries AD, what type of homes they built, the articles they used and the jewels they wore, so much of their lives appears at first to have vanished forever. Stone and rock do not easily disappear, but wood and cloth do not survive in the acid soil of Cornwall as they have sometimes survived in other Celtic areas of Europe. But if we cannot dig for more knowledge of their beliefs and lives, we can delve for it among the many writers from these countries who have left us their views of the Cornish at this time, given the close contacts between Cornwall and the rest of the world during the so-called Dark Ages. The growing number of remains discovered by archaeologists in recent years, together with the many legends attached to them, make this period of the story of the Cornish Celts no longer as distant and dark as once thought. The Celts had always passed on their history orally from generation to generation. Legends and beliefs have lingered longer in Cornwall than in many other parts of the country.

Celtic round houses can still be found today. In Veryan, near St Mawes, two pairs of whitewashed round houses, with thatched roofs and a cross at the top of each, stand guard at either end of the village. Another stands nearby on its own. They were built by a vicar, the Reverend Jeremiah Trist, in the early nineteenth century. He believed the round cottages would be ideal for agricultural labourers. The one high-ceilinged room would be healthy and easy to keep clean, and without stairs would be suitable for the elderly. Maybe this was also the belief of the builders of round houses since the Bronze Age. Alterations and extensions have been added to the cottages at Veryan, but they are still Cornish round homes. They are said to be round so that there were no corners in which the Devil could hide, and no north side by which he could enter. It was also thought that the houses pro-

Round house at Veryan, early 19th century.

tected the village against witches, for witches also hated houses without corners.

But, then again, there were other people who believed that the Devil kept away from Cornwall in any case, for fear of being made into a pie.

CHAPTER 2

Thoughts from Abroad

THE GREAT INTEREST shown in the Celts by Roman writers is surprising when we consider the little interest the Cornish Celts seem to have had in the Romans. In spite of the fact that they imposed their rule on the rest of Britain, the Romans left Cornwall comparatively undisturbed, describing it as on the edge of the habitable globe.

Whereas both ancient Greek and Roman writers tell us much of the background to the Celts, both in Europe and in Cornwall, the Celts themselves left no account of their lives before the writings of later Christian times which accounts, without doubt, were based on the stories they had been passing on orally for generations.

These stories were told round the family fireside and were of their heroes, their families and their history, later to be preserved and taught by the Druids, the priestly leaders of the tribes, who forbade any Celt to commit any of this knowledge to writing.

According to Julius Caesar the Druids originated in Britain and were a highly professional class who spent twenty years in training, committing their store of knowledge to memory. This they passed on to others in the Druidic schools of religious discipline, of which the most famous were in Britain and to which Celts from other countries came for training. They were the keepers of the history of the Celts and their complex laws, as well as performers of their priestly functions. They were natural philosophers and dealt with everything relating to the Celtic Gods. They not only committed the Celtic laws to memory but administered them as well.

There were three classes of Druids: those who engaged in the natural sciences and philosophy, including astronomy; those who performed sacrifices; and the bards, who were composers of poetry and songs, much like the bards of Wales and Cornwall today.

The early laws of the Celts show a compassion and understanding of human needs that is not apparent in the early accounts of their characters. Capital punishment was rare, but a murderer had to pay fines to the relatives and friends of the victim, so that a desire for vengeance was removed. Compensation to right wrongs was the usual punishment, although banishment to some other island was possible. To be forbidden from taking part in religious ceremonies was thought of as a severe punishment, perhaps the greatest of all.

The poor and the sick of the tribe laid claim to help from the strong and well-to-do. There was common ownership of land and goods, which was in conflict with the absolute ownership of property so important to the Romans. Their homes and family were a most important aspect of their lives, and ties of kindred were strong. The tribe was a larger version of the family, and the chief of the tribe was much revered and honoured. Tribe members, while bound to each other whether fighting or feasting, would follow their chief in battle without hesitation – a characteristic that the Cornish showed many times throughout history.

The Druids held the tribe together and their strict laws were severely enforced but, surprisingly, while a judge could be well paid for his services, if an appeal against one of his sentences succeeded and he was found to have given a wrong decision, he was branded on the cheek.

Notwithstanding this impression of the Celts and their leaders, the other side of their character was emphasised by many writers, and is the view that has endured in the public mind. The fact that they were head-hunters is not denied. The Celts believed that the human head was the seat of the soul. They cut off the heads of their enemies and nailed them over the doors of their homes and attached them to the necks of their horses as trophies. The ancient Greek writer, Diodorus Siculus says that they preserved in cedar oil the heads of the most important of their victims and kept them in wooden boxes. This may have been partly out of respect for their fighting prowess or as a means of possessing their souls. That they were fierce and frightening warriors when in battle is confirmed by many, but there is little evidence of this fighting in Cornwall, where the Celtic settlements were apparently peaceful farming communities. When they fought it is said that they fought naked, thickened and whitened their hair with lime, combing it to stand on end, and decorated themselves with blue woad, attacking savagely with much noise and shouting, adding to the effect on their enemies. The women of the tribes were as fierce as the men in battle, fighting alongside them. Their position in the tribe was important, and it was not unknown for them to be queens and leaders, for Roman writers noted that women were held in great respect. The Celt that is the best known to us is Queen Boudicca, described by a Roman historian as tall, terrible to look on, with a powerful voice, bright red hair down to her knees, and wearing a gold necklet, a multi-coloured robe and over it a thick cloak held together by a brooch. 'She took up a long spear to cause dread in all who set eyes on her.'

When the battles were over, the Celts loved feasting and celebrating with heavy drinking. When they had won they gave the hero of the hour the choicest part of the meat being served. They were great hero-worshippers as well as ancestor-worshippers, as is shown in many of their epic poems and legends, which no doubt entertained them during the feasts. Diodorus wrote that, although they were generally clean-shaven, they had large drooping moustaches, which became entangled in their food as they ate and which acted as strainers when drinking. They wore astonishing clothes, dyed tunics and trousers, on top of which they sported colourful cloaks with patterns of small squares of every shade. These cloaks, made in Britain, were exported to Europe well into the Middle ages. That the Cornish Celts enjoyed feasting and drinking is confirmed by the discovery of beakers from which they drank mead made from honey, and from the remains of wine jars imported from Greece and Europe. That they loved pork we can see from the joints of pork often found buried with them in their graves, for a feast on their journey to the next world or perhaps to ensure that they could eat well when they arrived.

Sacrifice, animal and occasionally human was part of their lives, carried out by Druid priests. Whether or not these took place in the stone circles in Cornwall we do not know. Such rites were more likely to occur in the sacred woods and enclosures wherein lived the gods and spirits of trees and water, the objects of much devotion. On some sacred sites there are deep shafts containing the remains of customary votive offerings at shrines, with jewellery and pottery but also bones.

The shaft at St Erth, Penwith, was eleven metres deep. Only the Druid priests could offer sacrifice, and only through them could benefits be asked. The Celts were said by Caesar to be 'much given to religion'. Rivers, water and wells were of great importance, many thought to have divine and healing properties. Water was considered sacred as it was so essential to life.

Caesar said that the Druids taught that souls do not disappear but wander from one body to another. The Byzantine writer, Procopius, writing in the sixth century AD, tells a story of the people of Brittany conducting the souls of the dead to Britain in the middle of the night. They were awoken by knocking on the door and a low voice calling them to the seashore. There were boats laden with the souls of the dead, although they seemed empty, which they took on an hour's journey to Britain. On arrival they heard a voice calling the names of their passengers, but they saw no one. Whatever the sacred rites of the Celts, they always believed in the immortality of the soul.

According to the Roman writer Pliny, the Druids held a great feast on the sixth day of every month when, white-robed, they cut mistletoe from the trees, probably oak, with a golden sickle, laying it on white cloth, then sacrificed two white bulls. Pliny believed that the Druids were clever healers and that mistletoe was used to reduce blood pressure and treat ulcers – in fact, it was a remedy that was a cure-all. Mistletoe is a plant of legend because of its soothing and calming effect on the nervous system. In ancient herbal books it was often called 'the Golden Bough'. In treating the Celts, the Druids must have known of its calming properties over excited hearts.

Livy wrote that in war the Celts were 'given to wild outbursts and they fill the air with hideous songs and varied shouts'. He tells of 'the dreadful noise of arms as they beat their shields in some ancestral custom'. It is doubtful whether the mistletoe was enough to counteract this behaviour.

There were many other occasions for feasting and drinking during the year, with four particular dates for celebration. The first feast day was 1 February, a pastoral feast called Imbolc, connected with Brigit, a pagan goddess of fertility, whose feast day was allocated to St Brigid by later Christians. St Brigid was believed to have been the midwife to

Padstow festival in 1900

Mary at the birth of Christ, so invocations to her were plentiful when a woman was in labour. The second festival date was 1 May, known as Beltaine, again connected with the promotion of fertility, encouraging the crops and cattle to grow. This date is kept every year in Padstow when the town is decorated with flowers and greenery for the festival dance which involves the whole community, as well as the hundreds of visitors who come to watch and to take part in the ancient ceremony. They sing loudly as they follow the 'Obby Oss' round the quay and up through the town.

Another spring festival is held on 8 May at Helston, on the Lizard peninsular, when the Furry dance is enacted through the main streets with couples dancing in and out of houses along the way.

By 1 August, the feast of Lughnasa, the Celts were ready for another celebration. This was not so much a pastoral feast but more to help the harvesting of crops, and originally the Celts managed to extend the feasting for a month. In Christian times the harvest festivals took the place of the pagan feast which had been in honour of the god Lugus or Lugh.

The last festival of the pagan Celtic world, the feast of Samain, was held at the end of the Celtic year and the beginning of their new year

Helston Floral Day in 1910

on 1 November. The celebrations started the night before and all the forces of magic and the supernatural were thought to be involved. The ancient Celts had always believed that the spirit world was very close to the human world and that it was possible to stray from one to the other, sometimes by accident. This is illustrated in many Celtic folk tales around the world. The veil between the two worlds was considered to be especially easy to penetrate in certain places, especially on hilltops and in woods, and at certain times, such as the turn of the year. This was the time of Hallowe'en when the spirits could most easily slip through to the human world. The Christians made the first of November the feast of 'All Saints', or 'All Hallows', to counteract any unpleasant ghosts, goblins and witches that had been let loose the night before by a celebration for the many holy and good people in the world. It was followed by 'All Souls' day on 2 November when the Church prayed for the repose of the souls of the dead.

The Celts celebrated all their festivals with bonfires, and perhaps the bonfires and fireworks of 5 November, coming so soon after

Hallowe'en, are not just in remembrance of Guy Fawkes. The memories of many pagan festivals are long-lasting in the human mind.

Many parishes in Cornwall hold a feast day connected with the patron saint of their church. Apart from the services at the church on the Sunday, often workers and schoolchildren traditionally had a holiday on the following Monday. The whole weekend was filled with music, sport and feasting, with many variations from parish to parish. The Celtic sports of hurling and wrestling, with great competition between neighbouring parishes, took the place of more violent clashes between the tribes of earlier days. The need to express themselves with great activity, followed by even greater enthusiasm for feasting and drinking, was as strong as it had ever been.

The fascination of the Romans for the Druids waned by the first century AD and they made great efforts to eliminate both them and the Celtic religion. Pliny wrote that they were still active in Britain where 'they had penetrated the utmost parts of the earth'. The Romans implacably condemned human sacrifice by this time, and the fact that they believed the Celts still practised this, as well as the fundamental differences between the Celtic and Roman values and laws, was more than the Romans could tolerate.

New influences were to come into both Roman and Celtic lives with the coming of Christianity, and both cultures were to accept this and develop it in different ways. Eventually, however, both the Romans and the Druids were to lose their influence on Britain, although the Druids were to surface again in the sixteenth century.

When the Romans left Britain in the fifth century, their departure made little difference to the way of life of the Cornish Celts. They were happy and probably relieved to be able to continue the life they had enjoyed before the Roman occupation and which they had maintained with little difficulty while the Romans were present.

No doubt this was in some way due to the position of the peninsula, which had enabled the Cornish to develop in their own way, while the rest of Britain was still influenced by the remnants of Roman rule and vulnerable to attack by the Saxons. Even when Richard Carew was writing in the sixteenth century, he was able to describe how 'nature hath shouldered out Cornwall into the farthest part of the realm and so besieged it with the ocean' that it forms 'a demi-island in an island'.

In AD 410 Britain received the historic message from Rome that they must look after their own affairs and that henceforth the Romans would no longer be able to help them. When this message eventually reached the furthest corner of Britain, it was probably received with a touch of indifference by the Cornish, who were now free to continue the way of life they were experiencing four hundred years previously, just as if the Romans had never existed.

The rest of Britain had been greatly changed by the Roman way of living. They had so many reminders of the occupation, the roads, temples, villas and administrative organization the Romans had left behind. There was no going back to the past for them.

The Saxons had already infiltrated their midst, invited by the Romans in the first place, and they were soon to be overwhelmed by them.

The Cornish were upheld by the strong traditions of love of their land, their families and the growing influence of the saints who had brought the Christian religion to the county from Wales and Ireland, never to leave it. It was a religious strength that was to influence them in various forms throughout the centuries to come.

When eventually the Saxons fought their way across the south of England, coming dangerously close to the south-west, the Cornish found the one part of their beliefs and needs that was missing – a hero and leader for them to follow. This was to be a leader who would give them another four hundred years in which to carry on the Celtic way of life, a leader whose influence was not only to benefit the Cornish but to make things very difficult for the Saxons, until Christianity had spread over the country for Celt and Saxon alike. His name was to become familiar in much of the world through the centuries down to the present day – King Arthur.

If the land routes in and out of the county made contact with the eastern counties of England difficult, the sea and sea transport enabled visitors from Ireland and Wales to approach Cornwall more easily.

Much of our knowledge of these years comes not from Europe but from writers from these countries, whose people had been in contact with Cornwall for centuries, mainly through trade and through their search for the Cornish minerals, tin and copper, that had always attracted people to the county. Now they brought the Christian religion to Cornwall. The Welsh and Irish stories were handed down orally for many centuries and were not written down until the eighth and ninth centuries AD, but they tell of the lives of the Celts and of the early saints who visited Cornwall and left their names on many places all over the county.

It was these written words that were to bring the Druids back to public notice when they appeared in print for the first time in the sixteenth century. The stories of the Druids' activities fascinated the educated men of the time, even if they could only interpret what they read from their own viewpoint and knowledge. Without the benefit of the archaeological research of the present century to put the Celtic past into its historical context, their view of the behaviour of their primitive ancestors must have been something of a shock to an age in which knowledge of ancient history came for the most part from the Bible.

Later, the eighteenth century age of elegance and reason drew the Celts and the Druids into a romantic vision of the past, a vision that poets, writers and musicians up to the present day have done little to change.

It was this vision of the past which in the late seventeenth century assigned the Druids to Stonehenge, regardless of the fact that it was built some fifteen hundred years before the arrival of the Celts in Britain.

CHAPTER 3

Saints and Sinners

C HRISTIANITY CAME by sea to Cornwall, not from Rome, but brought to its shores in the fourth and fifth centuries AD by holy men from Brittany, Wales and Ireland. The people of these countries had been visiting the county for many years. This time it was not the search for land, tin, copper or gold which brought them, but the need to spread the Christian message. The Cornish Celts, with their constant interest in the spiritual side of life, were ready to embrace this message with passion and enthusiasm.

These 'saints', whose names are found all over Cornwall, were not necessarily canonized by the Church. The title was given to many holy men and women who were wise and devout in the pursuit of their religion in a variety of ways. These ways were often very different from the more rigid rules that were developing in the Church in Rome, with which the Celts were so often to clash. These saints were missionaries, and preferred a form of monastic worship and living that greatly appealed to Celtic souls. Meditation was at the heart of their practices. Often they lived the lives of hermits in isolation. They preferred small groups to large institutions.

Their missions would initially consist of a few huts, cells or 'lans', in an enclosure, round a small wooden church or oratory. This was often next to a well, which then became a holy site used for baptisms. The Celts had for long worshipped the spirits of these wells – water was considered sacred as it was so essential to life. Holy wells are found all over Cornwall and their waters were thought to have both magical and medicinal properties. Perhaps they are still, for many wells are being restored today. They can still be found often with votive rags tied to the trees and bushes that surround them. It is believed that when the rags drop off, the prayers will be answered. The water in the well at Madron is reputed to cure rickets. It has long been a place of pilgrimage.

Many of the parish churches of Cornwall stand on these earlier sites.

They still bear the names of the saints who converted the people of the surrounding district, baptizing them and healing them.

Legends abound as to their lives, not least as to how they arrived in Cornwall. That these courageous travelling men and women had arrived by boat was thought to be too simple an explanation for later generations to appreciate. There are stories of their arrival by more magical means – floating on a leaf, a mill stone, a stone coffin or a barrel. The idea of a floating leaf is not so unbelievable. A mode of water transport used in Wales and Ireland to this day is the coracle or currach, a wicker boat covered with skin, canvas or hide. It is capable of carrying several people. As many of the saints came in family groups, this method of transport may well have been used. A coracle lying low in the sea would look much like a leaf to the watchers on the shore. The other means of legendary transport may have been the very objects they brought with them, and arriving in Cornwall on a floating stone was not impossible. The bluestones of Wales were thought by some to have been brought to Stonehenge in Wiltshire by water, floating on rafts.

St Columba was said to have rowed from Ireland to found his monastic community on Iona in AD 563, with twelve companions in a currach. He landed there at a point known as 'Port na Curaich' (Port of the Currachs).

St Ia, who gave her name to St Ives, was the saint reputed to have come to Cornwall on a leaf. She arrived in the fifth century AD from Ireland. The king of that part of Cornwall was Theodoric, who massacred many of the early missionaries in about AD 460. St Ia was protected from this fate by a Cornish Chieftain, Dinan, who is said to have built a church for her on the headland at St Ives, where there is now a chapel dedicated to St Nicholas. She later built an oratory on the site where now stands the parish church of St Ia, built in the fourteenth century.

Her brother, St Erc (of St Erth), and another brother, St Euny, landed at Hayle, giving their names to villages nearby. St Erc was supposed to have died in 514 at the age of ninety, so these early saints must have been busy preaching and baptizing in the far west of Cornwall a century before St Augustine came from Rome to the east of England.

St Ia was eventually martyred by Theodoric, but by then she had left

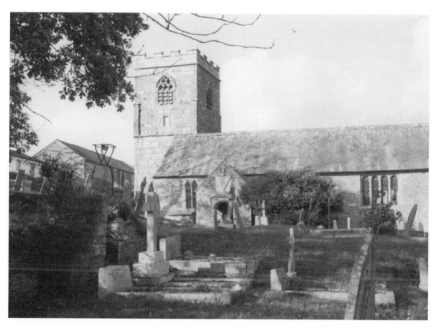

St. Sampson church

her name and her religion at St Ives for all time. She was described by William of Worcester, writing in the fifteenth century, as 'one of the chief virgins of the Sacred Isle'.

Hayle was a usual entry point for travellers from Ireland in prehistoric times, whence they travelled on a well-worn route to St Michael's Mount. This was the route for Irish gold and copper, which was traded for Cornish tin and then transported on to Mediterranean countries.

The earliest surviving biography of a Celtic saint is that of St Sampson, who came to Cornwall early in the fifth century. It was written about half a century after his death. Many of the lives of the saints of the fifth and sixth centuries were not written down until much later, so this life is more believable than most. Sampson was one of the most famous abbot-bishops of the early Celtic Church. He came to Cornwall from Wales and founded a monastery in the parish of St Sampson at Golant, near Fowey. He was said to have landed at Padstow and travelled with a wagonload of sacred books and holy vessels, leaving Cornwall at the end of his mission, probably from Fowey. This

Tristan Stone at Fowey, connected with the legend of Tristan and King Mark

Castle Dore hillfort, the legendary site of King Mark's castle

was a well-used route between Wales, Ireland and Brittany, where St Sampson next settled to found a monastery at Dol, where his life was later written and where he died a bishop in AD 565.

Today the church of St Sampson, which was consecrated in 1509, stands on the site of the ancient monastery. He is said to have first erected a shelter there near the well by the south door.

The church has strong associations with the stories of King Mark of Cornwall and the romance of his wife Iseult with his son Tristan. This was one of the great love stories of the Middle Ages. There are earlier references to it in Welsh and Breton sources, and the story has been told in many versions all over Europe, including the poems of Tennyson in the nineteenth century and Wagner's opera.

The nearby hillfort at Castle Dore has been identified as the likely home of King Mark. Nearby, the sixth century Tristan Stone now stands at the side of the road, a mile north-west of Fowey. It stands opposite the entrance to the former home of the late Daphne du Maurier, the author who did much to popularize the history and romance of Cornwall. On one side of the stone is a cross and on the other the inscription DRVSTANVS HIC IACIT CVNOMORI FILIVS (Drustanus lies here, son of Cunomorus). Cunomorus has been identified as Mark in a ninth-century manuscript, as the ruler of Cornwall and Brittany. Drustanus was the sixth-century version of Tristan's name.

Castle Dore was an Iron Age hillfort of around 200 BC, but its defences were reoccupied and extensively remodelled in the fifth century AD. Excavations have shown that, at this time, a timber-built hall twenty-seven metres by twelve metres was built along with other buildings. This hall is thought to have been the palace of King Mark. It had narrow aisles, with three bays, and a porch in front of the central bay. The twelfth-century poem by Beroul describes how the royal party visited the monastery of St Sampson, where Queen Iseult presented 'a garment of rich silk embroidered with gold; it was worth fully one hundred marks of silver and the like was never possessed by count or king'. The queen presented this dress as an offering on the altar. The poem tells how this was made into a priest's vestment, which was used once a year on the great anniversary of the saint's feast. The poem goes on to state, 'It is still kept in the church of St Sampson as those who have seen it bear witness.'

There are many legends connected with the activities of the saints in Cornwall and many versions of the best known of these legends, the story of Tristan and Iseult. Iseult was an Irish princess betrothed to

Pottery from Castle Dore with decoration in the style of Celtic design in the south west

King Mark. Tristan was sent by the king to escort her to Castle Dore, but unfortunately fell in love with her. He was forced to flee to France, where he became ill and died before Iseult could reach him. When she too died, they were buried together. The names of both Mark and Tristan occur also in many Welsh, Scottish and Breton romances, as was often the case with stories of the time. However, the Tristan Stone, the hillfort of Castle Dore with its wooden palace, and the nearby church of St Sampson give great credence to the legend that the story of the lovers may well have been enacted in Golant.

King Mark's hillfort again came into use in the Civil War, when a later king, Charles I, defeated the parliamentary forces in a decisive battle there on 31 August 1644.

St Petroc also came to Cornwall from Wales. He founded his first monastery in about AD 518 near Padstow (Petroc's stow, a church site). He had been educated at an Irish monastery and began his building with his band of followers – first a church, which he gradually enlarged into a Celtic monastery, with a school, infirmary, library, farm, and cells for the monks. He travelled widely in Cornwall, Wales and Brittany, founding other monasteries as he travelled. Eventually he returned to Cornwall and retired to a hermitage on Bodmin Moor at Bosvenagh ('the dwelling of monks'). When he died he was buried at first at Padstow, but later his relics were stolen away to Brittany, eventually, at the instigation of Henry II, to be brought back to Bodmin where they were contained in the painted ivory casket that is on display in St Petroc's Church there.

The patron saint of Cornwall is the sixth-century St Piran, who was also the patron saint of tinners. St Piran's Cross, a white cross on a black background, is on the Cornish flag. His relics were kept in a shrine at Perranzabuloe, which became an important place of pilgrimage, but these had disappeared by the beginning of the seventeenth century.

Many of the early monasteries, churches and holy wells were in the sheltered wooded valleys where the Celts had always loved to worship.

The local saints did not try to change the monastic and sometimes solitary aspect of the early Celts. They managed to adapt their Christianity to the ways of the Celts, ensuring a peaceful transition in their religious practices. All this displeased the Church in Rome, which

St. Piran's Cross mentioned in a charter of 960 AD

sometimes claimed that Cornish Christianity was simply a continuation of Druidism, but the authorities did not understand how close to nature it was. Living and working closely with the land and their animals, Cornish people were affected deeply by the seasons and the weather. They could not but be influenced by all that surrounded them. Their religion and prayers were part of their daily lives – seeing God in every plant, tree, bird in the air and star in the sky. Whether at work on land or sea, God and the saints were never far away from them. Their lives were hard and often dangerous and their religious beliefs needed to be strong to help them cope with whatever travails life brought. This was an aspect of the Cornish character which stood them in good stead, not only in ancient times but all through the centuries to follow.

Their prayers covered every act of their day, on the farm or in the round of their domestic duties, large or small, with a variety of saints called on to help at every turn.

The Irish Celt Pelagius was preaching the doctrine of free will in Rome, and this cult spread to Britain. He stated that man was responsible for his own acts and could overcome evil by his own strength, a doctrine that must have appealed to the Cornish. For this he was attacked by St Augustine, who preached that everything was pre-ordained by God, and that temptation could only be resisted with the help of the Church. Pelagius argued that this would encourage men to sin and to abdicate moral responsibility for their own acts. For this he was declared a heretic, which distanced the Celtic Church further from Rome for many years. Britain was thought of as the final stronghold of this heresy. In 429 the Pope sent Germanus to Britain to uproot this evil.

But there is no suggestion that Germanus had to combat paganism as well as to put down the Pelagan heresy.

The Celtic clergy shaved the front of their heads instead of the top as did the Romans. They celebrated Easter on a different day to the Roman Church. Only when King Athelstan created a diocese of Cornwall with a bishop at St Germans in the tenth century did Cornwall begin to conform. This was not because people did not know what was going on in Rome. The lives of the saints show that they made many early visits to Rome. They just did not wish to conform, but preferred to develop in their own way. British bishops had attended the Council of Arles in AD 314 and one at Rimini in 359. Final reconciliation with Rome came at the Synod of Whitby in AD 664, though independent Celtic Christianity lingered for many years.

The early Irish and Welsh saints introduced the first writing to Cornwall by means of the Ogham script, which consisted of strokes cut at varying angles. It first appeared in Cornwall on the memorial stones, found around the county, usually to commemorate a local ruler, often a Christian ruler. Often they display the Chi-Rho monogram forming the Greek initials of Christ. A group of the Ogham stones is to be found in north Cornwall, where it is thought there was an Irish settlement in about AD 500. One such stone of sixth or seventh century date stands at a crossroads between St Endellion and Portquin. It is sometimes called the Long Cross or Brocagnus Stone. One inscription underneath a Chi-Rho monogram reads BROCAGNI HIC IACIT NADOTTI FILIVS (Brocagnus lies here, the son of Nadottus). This is repeated in the Ogham script. On the back of the stone is a cross carved in relief. Another stone with an inscription in both Latin and Ogham is in the churchyard at St Kew. Evidence of settlers from Ireland also comes from pottery found here. There is an unbroken sequence of hand-made pottery from Iron Age times. This was interrupted in the sixth century by the appearance of straight-sided pots with finger-pinched decoration along the rims. These are known as 'grass-marked' pottery, from the marks left on the bases when they were rested on grass to dry before being fired, leaving the grass imprint on the underside.

There were so many saints arriving in Cornwall from Ireland at this time that there may be some connection between this type of pottery and their arrival. After all, it is unlikely that St Ia arrived at St Ives without her essential pot for cooking, eating from, or even for bailing out her coracle.

A settlement of peasant farmers has been extensively excavated at Gwithian, north of Hayle, on the west Cornish coast. In the fifth century there was only one hut here, the inhabitants using pots that were hand-made copies of Roman ware. By the sixth century there were three huts, the owners using grass-marked pottery. This type of pottery continued to be used in Cornwall until the eleventh century.

Sherds of this pottery were found with household refuse on the Gwithian site that had been spread as manure over fields. The fields had been dug with a plough with a coulter and fixed mould-board of a type developed by the Romans. The actual turned furrows in the sandy soil were revealed in the excavation by contrasting layers of sand and soil.

Pits of this household waste on the settlement showed that the inhabitants ate quantities of shellfish, as was to be expected on this coastal farm, but also beef, mutton and pork. The remains of a rotary quern were also found. The pig was an animal greatly revered by the Celts, who were said by classical writers to prefer it to other meat. They hunted and ate the wild boar, and salted it for the winter. The hunt of this animal features in many early Celtic stories. Joints of pork were found among goods in early Celtic graves to provide for the inhabitants' journey to the next world.

Many of the stones found in north Cornwall may have been prehistoric, with Christian inscriptions carved later. St Patrick was said to have cut a cross on a stone venerated by earlier Celts to turn it from pagan to Christian. There is a gap in Cornwall between the early inscribed stones and the free-standing stone crosses that are found later in the ninth and tenth centuries. Cornwall has more of these than any other county. Many are as late as the eleventh or thirteenth centuries. They were erected in churchyards; some mark the pathway to a parish church. Many of the most skillfully carved crosses are in the areas of Bodmin Moor and Land's End, where local monasteries may have had schools of sculpture attached to them. Carving the hard granite must have made intricate patterns difficult to produce, but two have the name Runhol inscribed on them. One is now in the garden of the convent at Lanherne, St Mawgan. It had formerly stood in the parish of Gwinear. The other is at Sancreed, where there are two crosses in the churchyard. The one near the south porch has the name Runhol on it. Both these crosses have the figure of Christ carved on them and are decorated with patterns of the tenth century.

Two of the best examples of crosses often known as 'high crosses' are in the churchyard of the fifteenth century church at Cardinham. Nearby, the powerful medieval family of Cardinham lived in their twelfth-century castle, but the two inscribed stones of the sixth and

Cardinham Cross

seventh centuries are not far away, showing a long period of occupation of this area from the earliest Celtic times.

The coastline of Cornwall is forever changing. The sea level rises, the sand dunes advance, the estuaries silt up. Towns that were originally ports are found today many miles from the sea. The church of St Piran has been buried in sand dunes since 1804. But a cross still stands nearby, mentioned in a charter of 960. The relics of the saint were kept in the oratory of St Piran nearby, an important place of pilgrimage in the Middle Ages, before it too was buried in the sand. It was excavated in the nineteenth century, but had to be reburied in 1981 to preserve its structure. A memorial stone marks the spot. The church stood in a large churchyard, the outline of which can still be seen. This may have been the enclosure of the original monastery of St Piran.

The church of St Enodoc at Trebetherick was much loved by the poet Sir John Betjeman, and his resting place is in the churchyard there. This church was also partly buried for many years in the sand dunes and accessible only through a hole in the roof. It was restored in 1873 and is now visited by many of the poet's admirers, having featured in his Cornish poetry.

The sea and the weather have always had a great effect on Cornwall, a county described by Bishop Grandisson of Exeter in the fourteenth century as 'not only the ends of the earth, but the very end of the end thereof'. And he was only looking at it from nearby Exeter! Those who travelled to Cornwall from distant lands across the seas were made of sterner faith.

CHAPTER 4

Mists and Legends

THE BELIEF of the Celts that hill-tops were special places for meetings between this world and the spirit world makes it not surprising that the most spectacular Cornish mountain, St Michael's Mount, overlooking Mount's Bay in the Land's End peninsula, has such a long and fascinating history, both religious and secular.

The religious history of the mount begins in the fifth century AD when St Michael was said to have appeared to some fishermen, who saw him standing on a ledge on the rock high above the sea. This was 'The great vision of the guarded mount', a line in Milton's poem *Lycidas*. This vision made the mount a place of veneration for centuries, an inspiration to priests, pilgrims and poets. But no doubt pagan Celts had venerated the hilltop long before recorded history.

In Iron Age times the mount had been a port of importance for traders from Ireland, coming to Cornwall for Cornish tin, which was then exported by sea and land routes as far as the Mediterranean. The mount was probably the island of 'Ictis' mentioned by the Greek writer Diodorus Siculus, writing in the first century BC in connection with the Cornish tin trade. The tin at this time was most likely shipped to France by the Veneti tribe of Brittany. They were a strong seafaring people who sailed in light, fast ships. Only when the Veneti were defeated by the Romans, who by then had discovered other sources of tin, did the Cornish trade decline somewhat.

However, the story of the Mount goes even further back than the traders, further back than the saints, in fact back to the age of legends when the rock was said to have been built by the giant Cormoran, who constantly raided the mainland for sheep and cattle to take back to his home on the mount. This he did not only for food but to increase his wealth, not with money or gold, but with what was of greater wealth to a Celtic farmer – cattle. Jack was a local Cornish boy who rowed out to the mount at night to prepare a deep pit as a trap for the giant, halfway

St. Michael's Mount

up the hill. When it was finished, the giant was awoken suddenly in the morning by the sound of Jack's horn. He was blinded by the bright sunlight when he rushed down the hill, and fell into the pit to his death. The hero Jack was given the title 'Jack the Giant Killer' by the grateful local inhabitants.

Across the Channel was another mount, Mont St Michel, very like the Cornish mount, but on a grander scale. It stood in a small bay between Brittany and Normandy. There too there had been visions of St Michael. He appeared to the abbot there in 708 and commanded him to build a sanctuary, later to be a Benedictine monastery. This was founded by Richard I in 966, with a great church completed in 1136. It became a noted centre of learning and, after the Norman conquest, Reginald, Earl of Cornwall, established a religious community on the Cornish mount with close connections between the two. The Cornish Benedictine priory there was built in 1135 and enjoyed a long and varied history. By the reign of Henry V, England was at war with France and the king granted the mount to Syon Abbey at Twickenham, severing its bond with Mont St Michel.

At the time the priory was being built, the twelfth century parish church of St Materiana was built high on the clifftop, overlooking Tintagel and its island. This saint appears to be one of the few saints in

Cornwall of whom we have little knowledge. Mists so often hide the castle and the island from view that it is not surprising that the early history of this small church is not as straightforward or clear as it seems. The saint to whom the church is dedicated could, it is thought, be either male or female.

Everyone who has visited Tintagel over the centuries has managed to see what they wanted to see and believe what they wanted to believe. Only in this century have archaeologists begun to sort out fact from fiction. They still have a great deal to unearth, but it is doubtful that they will ever completely dispel the strong feelings of mystery the place inspires in all who go there. If there is magic at work anywhere in Cornwall, it is surely at Tintagel, and it is unlikely that any scientific facts will be powerful enough to destroy it.

Around the cemetery visible today, there are signs of what was a pre-Norman enclosure, found on many early Christian sites and known as a 'lann'. As well as the original cemetery and a nineteenth-century extension, there are several grassy mounds, also in the enclosure. Evidence has now been found for the existence of a cemetery beneath the present churchyard. When digging new graves, the gravediggers came upon the remains of earlier cist burials. These are slate-lined graves similar to those at Harlyn. This earlier cemetery extends outside the area of today's churchyard. Some of the graves contained the remains of skeletons. One of the grassy mounds was excavated and found to contain an unusual cist without a burial. If the other mounds are found to contain similar individual burials, it is likely that this was a special burial place for the most important people on the island during the period from AD 450 to 600. Whoever they were, they were not buried on the island, where the chapel of St Juliane is of much later date, built probably about the same time as the parish church.

It is now believed that local rulers occupied what was a formidable citadel on the island from the fifth to eighth centuries AD. There were over seventy rectangular buildings, supplied with water from at least six springs or wells. This was not a religious community as at one time thought. These were people of considerable wealth and power, who were able to import large amounts of pottery and other wares in the sixth century AD, more than has been found at any other site of this date in Britain; some of it came from the eastern Mediterranean, and included shards of pottery from North Africa. There were large containers for wine and oil. Similar pottery of the same date has also been found on other sites in Cornwall, Somerset, Wales and Glastonbury. All these are places connected with the name of King Arthur.

The pottery may have been landed on this seemingly unapproachable island at a small landing place on the east side, used in medieval times, and where this sixth-century pottery has also been found. Sea levels rose by the end of the Roman period, and in the twelfth century Geoffrey of Monmouth wrote that the isthmus joining the island to the mainland was 'so narrow that three armed knights might hold it against the entire realm of Britain'.

The name of King Arthur has been associated with the castle on the mainland for centuries. Unfortunately, he has now been identified by both historians and archaeologists not as a king but as a military leader, of the fifth century AD, long before the castle whose remains are seen today was built. At least he has now emerged from the realms of pure fiction. Tintagel Castle, which stands partly on the mainland and partly on the island, was built by Richard, Earl of Cornwall, the brother of Henry III, in 1230. The castle has been owned by more than twenty successive earls and dukes of Cornwall. It is still held by the present duke and administered by English Heritage.

By the time it was built, the association of Tintagel with early stories of King Arthur was becoming known all over Europe. It is thought this inspired Richard to enhance his personal recognition by building his castle at Tintagel. He constructed his great hall over the court of the previous owner, and from this moment the stories multiplied.

When any constraints that had been imposed on them by both the Druids and the Romans faded in the fourth and fifth centuries, the Celts experienced a great sense of freedom. In Wales and Ireland they began to put down in writing (this had been forbidden by the Druids) the stories that had been handed down orally round Celtic firesides for generations. These stories mostly take the form of poems of praise and celebration. Those by the Welsh poets Taliesin and Aneirin are among the oldest. Aneirin's poem 'Gododdin', dating from AD 600, contains the oldest literary allusion to Arthur. He says of one of a group of nobles fighting the Saxons at Catterick that his valour was great 'although he was no Arthur'. The poems do not give a clear storyline; they obviously assumed that the audience was well aware of the details. They give a general feel, with vivid pictures of events of the times, both heroic and tragic.

It is from these early stories passed on by minstrels and missionaries from Wales, Brittany and Cornwall that the legend of the king who had defeated the enemies of the Celts in the sixth century spread throughout Europe.

When the historian William of Malmesbury visited Glastonbury Abbey in Somerset in about 1125, he was told stories of the early years of the history of Britain, when the community of the abbey was already in existence and when the stories of Arthur were taking form. The stories made such an impression on William that, when he came to write his *Deeds of the Kings of the English* that year, he said that Arthur was clearly a man worthy to be proclaimed in true histories, not 'fallacious fables'.

William also recorded the devotion of Irish pilgrims coming to Glastonbury to venerate the relics of saints kept there. It was usual in the sixth century for important chieftains or warriors to be buried near the graves of saints. The Celtic belief was that the graves of such leaders gave protection to the land where they were buried. This further encouraged the belief in the legend that Arthur was buried at Glastonbury. It also adds weight to the importance of whoever was buried in the grassy mounds in Tintagel churchyard, in view of the long history of the site.

The next history of the kings of Britain was written soon after William's by an ecclesiastic, Geoffrey of Monmouth. His book became the chief source of the Arthurian stories of the Middle Ages. He claimed to have based his book on Welsh monastic writing, poems and legends, and on Breton folklore. He brings the name of Arthur into his history of England, as the child of Uther Pendragon and Ygerne, born at Tintagel. Ygerne's husband was Gorlois, Duke of Cornwall, and Tintagel was his fortress. Uther deceives Gorlois by impersonating him with the help of the wizard Merlin, and marries her after her husband dies in battle. In Geoffrey's version, their son, Arthur, succeeds to the throne while young and starts his campaign against the Saxons, who have invaded Britain, beating them back at the Battle of Badon. Here, according to Geoffrey, he is helped by his sword Caliburn, made in Avalon, and his spear called Ron, an unlikely name, but Geoffrey said it was long, broad in the blade and thirsty for slaughter. It graced his right hand. With his sword Arthur fought until he had killed 470 men in one battle. He marries a Roman lady, Ganhumara, and defeats the Saxons in Ireland, the Orkneys, Iceland, Norway and Gaul. No wonder his name is found today in so many parts of the world. According to Geoffrey, he ruled over the wealthiest, the most Christian and civilized part of Europe – Britain.

The Battle of Badon has been placed in various locations. The latest possibility suggested is Liddington Castle, a hillfort near Swindon, with a village called Badbury nearby. A hillfort at Badbury Rings in Dorset is another possibility. At this battle Arthur was said to have carried the cross of Jesus on his shoulders for three days and nights, and the Britons were victorious. At another battle, one of twelve he fought, he carried the image of the Virgin Mary on his shield. This decisive battle in which he defeated the Saxons is mentioned by many writers, though not by the *Anglo-Saxon Chronicle,* which is not surprising as he defeated the Anglo-Saxons and gave the west of England forty years of peace. Nine hundred and sixty men were said to have fallen in one day at Badon and 'no one overthrew them except himself alone'.

According to Geoffrey, Arthur was eventually wounded at the final Battle of Camlann in 538. He was carried away to Avalon to be healed of his wounds.

Although the king's knights had been mentioned in Geoffrey's history, as other writers took up the story the knights became larger than life, and the story developed in increasingly romantic ways. When a French version was presented by the poet Wace to Henry II's consort, Eleanor, in 1155, it featured the king's knights and also mentioned the Round Table. In the time of Henry II the knightly aspect of the story appealed both to the king and his court. Eleanor's daughter, by a previous marriage to Louis VII of France, had as her protégé Chrétien de Troyes, who wrote long poems of romance in the third quarter of the twelfth century. He set the court of King Arthur at Camelot and called his queen Guinevere. He linked her name with Sir Lancelot and brought in the story of Tristan and Iseult as well for good measure. In that age of chivalry and romance in Europe, his stories were immediate best-sellers in France, with versions soon appearing in Italian, German and Spanish. They developed into stories where the exploits of King Arthur were in the background and the stories of love and infidelity in marriage, together with courtly love outside it, were to the fore.

Alongside this aspect of the stories was a religious one. This involved the search for the Holy Grail. This was believed to have been a sacred vessel in pre-Christian Celtic myths. The story was elaborated in the thirteenth century, when the Grail became the chalice of the Last Supper. It was said to have been brought to Britain by Joseph of Arimathea, who was already connected with the legends of Glastonbury Abbey. He was thought to have visited England after taking possession of the body of Christ after the crucifixion, and to have founded the abbey at Glastonbury. Here he planted his staff to become the Glastonbury thorn, the tree that blooms at Christmas.

When Henry II visited the abbey he was told that the body of Arthur had been buried there. He suggested to the monks that they should search for it. Many believed that Arthur was not dead, but resting in a cave in some hidden hillside, along with his knights, and that he would rise again to come to England's aid if ever it was in danger.

Henry was anxious to prove that Arthur was really dead by finding his grave. Soon after the death of the king in 1190, diggers found a stone and a cross with a Latin inscription stating 'Here lies buried the renowned King Arthur in the Isle of Avalon'. Underneath was a large hollowed oak coffin containing the skeleton of a tall man with a badly damaged skull, together with some smaller bones and a scrap of yellow hair, thought to belong to his queen. The bones were put in a casket and kept with the abbey's treasures. In 1278 they were reburied in a new tomb in front of the high altar. This was still in place in the sixteenth century, but disappeared at the time of the Reformation. The site of the tomb was discovered in 1931, but only the base of the cavity remained. It was then grassed over and marked with a plaque.

At the time of the Third Crusade to the Holy Land, Richard I presented Tancred of Sicily with Arthur's sword, Excalibur, which he said had also been in the abbey. In Cornwall the legend is that the sword was thrown into Dozmary Pool, on Bodmin Moor, when Arthur was taken to Avalon after the battle.

With Tintagel connected with his birth and Glastonbury with his burial, it is not surprising that these two places have become so associated with the legends connected with Arthur.

A complete Arthurian cycle was produced by Sir Thomas Malory during the Wars of the Roses in the fifteenth century. These romantic stories were edited by William Caxton and printed by him for the first time in 1485 as *Morte d'Arthur*. It was Malory who wrote the words 'The Once and Future King' that have been associated with the name of Arthur ever since. These stories, like Geoffrey of Monmouth's history, were a great success. With Malory, the Holy Grail became the object of the quest by Arthur's knights.

The flow of Arthurian magic continued in the seventeenth century, when Henry Purcell wrote the music for an opera entitled *King Arthur or The British Worthy*, which was produced in March 1691 at London's Dorset Garden Theatre, with a libretto by John Dryden.

It was Alfred Lord Tennyson, Poet Laureate in the reign of Queen Victoria, who rewrote the stories yet again for the Victorians, including the queen herself. He dedicated his 'Idylls of the King' to the memory of the tragedy in the queen's own life of the death of her husband, Prince Albert, in 1861. Tennyson revived interest in the Arthurian stories in the nineteenth century. They were read by millions and laid the groundwork for the many treatments since, by writers, artists and composers from Walt Disney to Wagner, with his opera *Tristan and Isolde*, and Lerner and Lowe's *Camelot*. It seems there is no limit to what can be newly discovered by all who come into contact with the king.

If we cannot see a plaque at Tintagel island stating that King Arthur was born there, folklore has added his name to many features on the rocks there. We can find King Arthur's seat, his window, and his cups and saucers (the eighteen or so small circular holes in one of the rocks which appear to be man-made). Then there is the cave on the shore of the island where Merlin is supposed to have found the baby Arthur. The most interesting of these features is King Arthur's footprint, made, the legend says, when he stepped in one stride across the sea to Tintagel church. The footprint is on the highest point of the island, on a slate shelf, with a wonderful view of both the church and the ancient burial ground on the mainland. It is a small hollow in the shape of a human foot, twenty-three by forty-three centimetres.

The Celts believed that such a footprint on a rock marked the place where a chieftain or king was required to stand, during a recognised ritual, when claiming possession of a site. The Tintagel footprint may be entirely natural or may be a natural hollow altered in its early history to form the footprint. However, its appearance in a place with such a background merely adds to the hope that the legend that King Arthur's palace once stood on Tintagel island may yet be proved true.

CHAPTER 5

Arts and Artisans

THE CELTS in general are thought of as a people linked by religion, speech and culture, not by economics or politics; but the Cornish Celts have always developed a strong economic edge to their character, owing to the unique environment in which they lived. The minerals and metals that attracted others to them, combined with their own knowledge and mining skills, enabled them to both trade in these basic materials and to fashion articles from them to make everyday objects for their own use and eventually for the use of others.

The stone axes they made in the beginning they eventually made to be used in many parts of the country, following on from the flint tools of earlier man. It is possible that they first made religious objects of wood which have now perished. Carved images of their gods have been found, but early stone carvings are rare in Cornwall. Their use of stone was primarily dedicated to the building of their homes, stone circles and burial chambers.

With the coming of the Iron Age the blacksmith enjoyed an exalted position, and became one of the most important people in Celtic society. He fashioned the tools with which they worked and, most important, the weapons with which they fought. If these objects were for practical use, the decoration on them was always of purely Celtic forms. The trade they had with different countries worldwide was for the most part thought to have been conducted by barter; the use of coinage came much later. The goods exchanged for Cornish tin brought a wealth of different styles of decoration to them. The Celts had the great ability to assimilate both these styles and the ideas that came with them into their own culture, and produce them in a unique Celtic form unlike that of any other culture in the world.

In the same way that their storytelling was not a straightforward narrative of events, but still managed to give listeners vivid pictures of what was happening to the characters portrayed, their art was also of a non-narrative quality. It did not tell a story or give a clear picture of the animals, birds or plants portrayed. These were there, but transformed to such an extent that only the idea of them remained in the Celtic vision.

They did not produce exact copies of designs that assimilated from other countries. These may have come to them from the Middle East, combined with ancient Greek and Etruscan influences, or from the Scythians. Some ideas and designs came across Europe from Austria and the early La Tène culture of western Switzerland and later from Rome.

As they worked and welded their metals, the Celtic crafstmen also welded all these influences into their own style, quite different from that of any in the Mediterranean classical world. However practical were the objects they made, the art with which they decorated them was abstract, non-representational, imaginative and magical. Their strong swords of iron had scabbards decorated with ornate designs in bronze. The natural surroundings they knew so well were there in forms that appealed to the senses of those who looked on them rather than to their minds. In spite of the strong physical aspects of the lives they led, human forms did not appear in their art, which was delicate, even fragile, showing clearly the many complexities of the Celtic character. The human head did, however, appear, but often only in the form of a mask. There are few portrayals of the Celts.

From the first they made decorative objects to ornament their persons. Whether or not these were first brought to Cornwall in exchange for Cornish tin is not certain. It is possible that travelling smiths from Ireland may have brought some of the gold objects found in Bronze Age burials. Golden torcs worn by men have been found in a Bronze Age burial at Harlyn and in a bog on a farm at St Juliot in Cornwall. They are of thin gold sheet with incised geometric patterns, made to Irish design, but it is believed from Cornish gold. Torcs could be either smooth or twisted with decorated terminals, sometimes solid or in two sections. One first-century AD bronze collar found at Lelant had a symmetrical stippled design with insets of clear and yellow glass. Thin torcs of twisted gold were found with gold bracelets to match. Finger rings were rarer. Bronze collars appear to have replaced gold torcs by the first century BC. By this date colour other than that of gold was becoming increasingly important, and enamelling in several colours was used in objects found in the British Isles.

Bronze mirrors of the last century BC have been found in women's graves in Cornwall, the backs decorated with engraved designs. These were objects not usually found on the Continent. Basketry decoration was hatched between curvilinear lines, made with the use of compasses; this had been a feature of the early La Tène period, but disappeared from later Continental Celtic material. It continued, however, to be a major characteristic of the work of Cornish metalworkers, and is fundamental to what is thought of as 'Celtic' design. This was the style of swirling spirals and scrolls developed further by the monks in the Christian period, who produced the wonderful illuminated manuscripts of the sixth and seventh centuries AD. It can also be seen on the pottery of this period in the south-west, as is evidenced by pots from the Castle Dore hillfort.

Much of early Celtic art featured not only on items that decorated their persons, but also on their fighting weapons, items so important to the warrior chiefs of the tribes, whether for actual fighting or as prestige items to be worn at ceremonial occasions. The ironsmiths often surpassed the art of the workers in gold and bronze with their work on swords and scabbards and on shield mounts.

In Cornwall the most usual objects found in graves of the early Celts and in rivers and wells are pins and brooches of the fourth and third centuries BC. The Cornish were at first more interested and occupied in the production of the actual metal for all these goods than in the finished designs. This was what they had become so skilled at during the previous centuries. As their production increased, a south-western style developed quite different from anything found on the Continent.

Settlements were found with huts once occupied by metalworkers where there were pits and hearths and stone moulds used for casting. At first single moulds were used for the early flat axes, but as more complicated tools and weapons were needed, two-sided moulds were used.

Bronze bowls sometimes found in bogs were probably votive offerings. They date from the first century BC. One found on a farm at Youlton in north Cornwall has an escutcheon of a grinning demon with

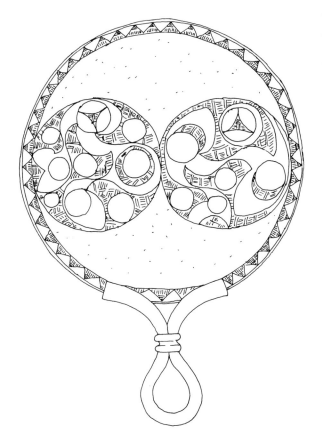

Bronze mirror from a woman's grave at St. Keverne. 1st century BC.

a plumed helmet. Masks of humans and animals were increasingly popular. Many of the objects of Cornish art have been found in rivers, streams and wells, left there as offerings to the gods, in particular the brooches that were an important item of Celtic dress. Often only the brooch is left in a burial, and the garment covering the body which it was attached to has rotted away. These scattered ritual deposits are hard to date. Some are thought to have been specially made as grave goods; many were most likely to have been wooden carvings which have long disappeared.

Decorative heads of dogs and boars are among the animal forms found, including bulls' heads decorating iron fire-dogs. The fire-dogs found among grave goods were included presumably to assist in cooking the feast the deceased expected in the next life.

Bronze bowl from a farm at Youlton. It has an escutcheon of a grotesque head with a plumed helmet.

The Romans' main interest in Cornwall was in the county's tin, which came increasingly under imperial control. It travelled to market in the form of ingots. A forty-pound tin ingot from St Mawgan had been stamped with an imperial inscription of the fourth century.

A fourth-century pewter jug from Halviggan, St Stephen-in-Brannel was found in a tin stream. A small pewter bowl found with it had been made from a larger vessel and had an inscription by Aelius Modestus dedicating it to Mars, the god of war and also of fertility.

As Celtic art declined in Europe, that of the south-western Celts of Britain developed and flowered. The Celts always had the ability not to copy but to adapt and assimilate, to transform and develop all the ideas and methods that came to them, from whatever source. This ability enabled them to continue assimilating both during and after the Roman period. The Christian period only enhanced this tendency, enabling them to put all their spiritual fervour into expressing their art in the articles they made.

The first stone carving in Cornwall seems to date from Roman times.

The large number of standing stones all over the county had been erected centuries before this, many as memorial stones to mark a burial, but without an inscription to indicate who was buried there. These uncarved stones appeared in the fourth to fifth centuries AD. It is possible that inscriptions and carvings were added to existing stones, especially if it became necessary to make pagan stones into Christian ones by the addition of Christian symbols. St Patrick has been described as cutting a cross on a stone formerly venerated by pagans.

In the porch of Phillack Church, near St Ives, is a small stone with the Chi-Rho symbol, of the fifth century, one of the earliest signs of Christianity in Cornwall. There is also a seventh-century stone marking the grave of Clotuali Mobratti here.

A fifth to sixth-century stone at St-Just in-Penwith has the inscription SENILUS IC JACIT (Senilus lies here) in Latin, also with a Chi-Rho cross (XP).

As the stoneworkers became more skilled in carving the hard Cornish granite, they decorated stones and crosses with the curves and knots of true Celtic design. One such stone and cross of the ninth century at St Cleer is known as King Doniert's Stone. It has an inscription in Latin, DONIERT ROGAVIT PRO ANIMA (Doniert has asked prayers for his soul). He is believed to have been a ninth-century king of Cornwall, who was drowned.

The many free-standing crosses of Cornwall, more than are found in any other county, are mostly dated from the ninth century, and many of them are from the later Norman period, when they are found in churchyards, many marking the way to the parish church.

Monasteries at St Buryan and St Petroc at Bodmin may have had schools of sculptors attached to them, as so many of the most decorated crosses are in these areas. The crosses at St Buryan and those in the churchyard at Sancreed have the first carvings of the robed figure of Christ worked into the designs. Crosses with wheel-head tops became well established in Cornwall. The wheel was a symbol of the sun in pagan Celtic times. The crosses at Sancreed and the cross at Lanherne are the only two that have the name of the sculptor, 'Runhol', carved on them.

There are some stones in the Penwith peninsula that have holes

The Selus stone from St. Just church, 5th century AD with Chi-Rho sign

rather than carvings in them, and these have not been explained. The row of stones with small holes in them near St Just at Kenidjack are such a mystery. The hole in the Mên-an-Tol stone, north of Lanyon Quoit, is larger, large enough for a naked child to be passed through. It is said to cure rickets.

Some evidence that the Romans intended to make a road in Cornwall, probably for the movement of tin, is found in the five milestones they left behind. One dating from AD 250, is at Tintagel Church and acts as part of the churchyard entrance, with an inscription to the Emperor Caesar Gaius Valerius Licinius. Another is at Breague churchyard, and is the only surviving stone dedicated to the Emperor Postumus. These milestones, together with one at Trethevey and one at St Hilary, mark the route to Land's End and St Michael's Mount, whence travellers journeyed to the Continent.

The St Hilary stone is 1.3 metres high with ten lines of inscription in Latin which state, 'In the reign of Emperor Flavius Valerius Constantinus, pious, noble Caesar, son of the divine Constantinus Pius Augustus'. The milestone is dated AD 306–8.

Like all the milestones it fails to indicate where the road is leading (possibly not to Rome) or how far it is to the next destination.

CHAPTER 6

Castles and Kings

WHEN ST AUGUSTINE began the conversion of the Saxons of eastern England in AD 597, Celtic Cornwall had already been converted by the saints from Ireland and Wales who had come to the county in the fourth and fifth centuries. This part of the Church was still mainly independent of Rome. The Synod of Whitby in AD 664 still left Cornwall opposed to the order and formal organization of the Church. The outward reasons for nonconformity may have been disagreements as to the date of Easter, or the method of shaving the heads of the clergy, but the real reasons were the Celtic Church's wish to be free of restrictions, while still being deeply Christian. There was a difference in outlook as to the possession of land. Celts thought of a bishop holding land as head of a clan, limiting it to that around his monastery, not to a wider territory.

By the year 710 Exeter was in Saxon hands, but the Saxon rule did not extend to Cornwall, except to the far eastern side of the county. For four hundred years the Romans had not greatly influenced Cornwall, and for the next four hundred years the county was not greatly influenced by the Saxons.

It was in the ninth century that Cornwall was eventually conquered by Egbert, but from this time another influence was affecting England. The threat of the Danes or Vikings came gradually nearer to Cornwall, reaching the eastern side of the county by the time of King Alfred. The Danes had settled in Normandy across the English Channel, whence they could harass the coastal regions of the south and Cornwall. The obviously nervous Cornish clergy buried valuable treasures at this time. Some was found in 1774 in an old tin stream at Trewhiddle, near St Austell, never to be recovered by the Church. The hoard of silver objects dating from the ninth century was Saxon, not Celtic; the Saxon influence had now reached the churches in this part of Cornwall.

By 931 King Alfred's grandson Athelstan had brought all Cornwall under English rule and created the diocese of Cornwall, with its first bishop at St Germans. From this time many monasteries became churches with canons instead of monks. By the time of Athelstan's death in 939 the Celtic Church was under the rule of the bishops enforcing the rules of Rome.

Under Ethelred in 978 the Danes rose again. The Danish fleet sacked Padstow and the monastery of St Petroc was transferred to Bodmin. The only Cornish book to have survived was written in the ninth or tenth century, probably in France. It was the Bodmin Gospels, which contained entries relating to the freeing of slaves, mostly with Celtic names, in ceremonies of manumission. The lowest classes in Celtic times were often considered as slaves, and were sometimes used by the Celts as barter for luxury goods, a practice that continued in Saxon times.

The first stone crosses and early churches date to this period. By 1040 Cornwall had lost its own bishop at St Germans; the diocese was combined with that of Devon, and the see was moved to Exeter, where it remained for eight hundred years until the formation of the diocese of Truro in 1876.

The Saxons had already taken over the local government of the county, substituting their feudal system for the Celtic tribal forms of ownership of land. This was now divided into hundreds and then manors. The old tribal centres became the new manors. The Saxon 'tun' was added to Celtic place names, Henlis becoming Helston. The Celts still preferred to live in isolated farms, many identified by the Celtic prefix of 'tre'.

The conquest of the country by William in 1066 brought further changes in organization which the Celts of the far west could not fail to see. The visible signs of the presence of the Normans were not easy to ignore.

Under the Normans every holder of land was to be the tenant of his feudal superior and every man was to have his lord. The ownership of the land was now vested in the king. He ordered the Domesday survey of 1086, a detailed survey of all William now owned in his new kingdom. The Saxons who had dispossessed the Celtic chiefs were now replaced themselves by French-speaking Normans. The clergy spoke

Latin and only the lower classes in Cornwall, the majority of the people, spoke Cornish. Soon the Church and monasteries were under Norman control. Some of the latter were reorganized under a new order of Augustinian canons, who built a new church at Bodmin. Launceston Priory and St Germans also acquired new churches. The Normans enjoyed a higher standard of life in their monasteries than they found in those in Cornwall. Accordingly many changes were soon made. A prior and twelve monks were sent from Mont St Michel to the new Benedictine monastery at St Michael's Mount, and the church there was consecrated in 1135. At Tywardreath, near St Austell, another Benedictine priory with French connections was founded at the same time.

The most visible signs of the Norman conquest in Cornwall were the Norman castles.

The term 'castle' has been applied to various defensive fortifications of prehistoric and Celtic times in Cornwall, such as the cliff castles and hillforts, but the first castles as we usually think of them – large, for-bidding edifices in stone – were not built until after the Norman con-quest. The first fortifications put up by the Normans, hoping to impress on the local inhabitants the fact that they were well and truly conquered, were mostly built of wood. But soon the early stone castles, at Cardinham, Tintagel and Restormel (near Lostwithiel), not mentioned in the Domesday survey, were built after 1085.

Needless to say the Cornish people were not fond of either the Norman barons or their castles, and the term 'castle' was often used in a derisory sense to describe houses built in a pretentious style, as the term 'folly' might be used in other parts of the country.

Whatever the Cornish may have thought of them, it was impossible for them to ignore the Normans or their castles. They did bring an order and organization to Cornwall which was more lasting and stronger than anything that had gone before. Towns such as Truro became boroughs and could manage their own affairs independent of the manor of which they formed a part. The king's authority was further extended over the country by travelling justices. In Cornwall the assize court was held at Launceston. All males were made liable for military service, but no man was liable for service outside his own county. The

Cornish were anxious to take advantage of this rule in the civil war of the seventeenth century.

King John obviously realized the importance of the tin industry to the Cornish. He issued the first known charter to the ancient Stannaries in 1201, confirming the tinners' rights and privileges, including their right to search and dig for tin on unenclosed common land, even to divert any stream for their use. The tinners had their own stannary courts and parliament, which could impose heavy penalties on those who broke their laws. Lostwithiel was a stannary town. The tinners had to bring their metal to be weighed and stamped. Failure to keep the laws resulted in imprisonment in Lostwithiel gaol.

Richard, the second son of King John, was granted the county of Cornwall and its tin works in 1225 and was made Earl of Cornwall two years later. His son, Edmund, succeeded him on his death.

An early castle would consist of a mound with a wooden keep or tower on its flat top, later to be replaced by a stone tower, often the only part of the castle still remaining today. This was built when the mound, if man-made, had settled enough to stand the weight of the huge structure to be erected on it. Around this mound was the bailey, an area surrounded by a stockade, inside which all the activity of the castle took place. William the Conqueror made his half-brother, Robert of Mortain, the first Earl of Cornwall, and it was he who refortified the early timber palisades of Launceston and Trematon with stone walls. At Launceston the builders could take advantage of a partially natural hilltop, where there had been some sort of fortification before the conquest with the ancient name of Dunheven.

It was the stone tower which, in time of trouble, was the last refuge of the inhabitants of the castle, and was at first known as the 'donjon', later to become the dungeon. As it was often used as a prison, being the strongest part of the castle, a dungeon came to mean a prison in the lower regions of the keep, where there was no way out or means of entry from the outside. In the sixteenth century the dungeon tower became the keep, a term that lingered on in the 'keeping' rooms of the early settlers in America and later in the parlours or best living rooms of nineteenth century cottages, known as 'keep' rooms. The word 'motte' was at first applied to the mound on which the keep stood and

Launceston Castle in 1876

later became the 'moat', a word for the ditch around the mound, formed when the mound was erected.

The Norman castle, as well as being a military centre in a male-dominated society, was also a home for the nobleman's lady, her family and her women retainers. They were often housed in the top floor of the keep, the only part of the tower that was considered safe enough to have slightly larger windows, giving it the name of the 'solar' or sun room, a name that also attached itself to the private living room of the nobleman in his hall. This hall was often situated in the castle grounds. The private family living room in the later manor houses was also called the solar. Somewhere in the tower would be the wardrobe – not then a cupboard, but a room or rooms where, as well as robes, spices, plate and jewels were stored. Only when homes were scaled down did it become a mere cupboard.

One advantage in living at the top of the tower must have been the comparative peace and quiet there compared with the tumult that prevailed in the lower quarters and the castle grounds. The noise must have been unbearable – the clang of armour and the activity of blacksmiths, cooks, carpenters and stonemasons – for the bailey contained all the buildings for the maintenance of the castle and its occupants. Excavations in the bailey at Launceston have shown a great density of occupation by the late eleventh century, with rows of stone houses probably intended for the housing of the castle guard. The buildings were laid out symmetrically on an internal street plan. To be housed at the top of the keep might have been no bad thing with so much going on below, although if the castle was under siege and the action was taking place on the roof the situation would have been different. There was often also a chapel in the bailey, and this was usually one of the first buildings to be built in stone.

As time went on, castles also became centres for the administration of justice. When Launceston Castle was reorganised and refortified in the mid-thirteenth century, during the earldom of Richard of Cornwall, the great hall was built near the south gate in the bailey wall, the fourth building to occupy the site. It continued as the assize hall until about 1600. It was originally a ground-floor building, perhaps with a screen at one end, and it was converted in about 1300 to a first-floor hall with a fireplace. This was probably done when Edmund, Earl of Cornwall, reduced the status of the castle and transferred its administrative functions to Lostwithiel, leaving it as the centre for the administration of justice.

At first any improvements made to a castle were not designed for the comfort of the inhabitants, but rather involved strengthening the walls, entrances and towers or designing more effective arrow-loops, the narrow slits in the walls through which the defenders could shoot at the enemy, hopefully without being seen. Safety was more important than light, although in view of the fact that there was no glass in the windows, small windows were an advantage. Head-dresses were always worn and garments were long and draught-proof for men as well as women. There were few concessions to easy living. Staircases were not designed for gliding down in these long dresses, but were steep, narrow and winding so that they could be easily defended.

Launceston Castle was described in 1602 as having a steep, rocky-footed keep surrounded by a treble wall and even then was known as 'Castle Terrible'. The innermost wall was three metres thick and about fifteen metres high. The wall surrounding it was between three and 3.6 metres thick and about nine metres high, and surrounding this was a third wall, 800 millimetres thick and two metres high. All these walls were battlemented.

The space in the centre of the keep was about six metres in diameter and was roofed over. It contained the Earl of Cornwall's chamber and was warmed by a fireplace. A windowless dungeon was situated immediately below this room. Steps led from one floor to another, one flight of stairs leading to the guard tower, the ruins of which can be seen today. In the wall close to the guard tower was a doorway through which the inhabitants of the town could enter in times of trouble, reaching the keep over a drawbridge across the dyke surrounding the southern side of the castle. The remains of a chapel, the great hall, the constable's dwelling and the gaol are in the bailey. The infamous gaol stood on one side of the north-east gate and was a small chamber about 3.5 metres square where, among other unfortunates, the Quaker George Fox was imprisoned in the seventeenth century. He was later removed to Doomsdale, his name for an underground gaol beneath the prison proper where usually only the worst felons and condemned murderers were confined. The terrible conditions in which Fox was held eventually reached the ears of Oliver Cromwell, who obtained his release.

At Launceston there was a well dug into the inner slope of the motte ditch at an early date. A well providing fresh water for a castle was essential. Although water was not much used for drinking, it was used for cleanliness more than might be expected. There was usually a shaft built up through the thickness of the wall, with a small arched opening on to

Aerial view of Restormel Castle

each floor from where a bucket could be pulled up. Baths were taken in wooden tubs, but heating and carrying the water obviously involved great effort, although there would have been no shortage of manpower in a medieval castle. No doubt where there was a river nearby, it would have been used for washing clothes and for personal hygiene if the times were peaceful enough. The washing of hands before meals was considered essential. Servants carried water in ewers or 'aquamaniles' in the shape of animals; this was poured over the diners' hands and caught in a bowl underneath. The hands were then wiped on a towel, carried over the servant's arm. The same ritual was repeated at the end of the meal to clean greasy hands, as although knives and spoons were used forks were rare. Most civilizing influences in medieval times came from the Church, and the noble classes probably had a higher standard of hygiene then than in the centuries that followed. Life in the castles of the Middle Ages had a degree of civilization that had not been known before.

Starting the day with Mass in the chapel was part of the daily routine of almost everyone, which is why there would usually have been a chapel both in the keep and in the bailey. Only the humblest classes restricted their attendance to Sundays and feast days. Every castle and many a lesser dwelling had its chapel and chaplain, who also acted as secretary to the lord and as tutor to his children.

The only female servants were the lady's waiting women, the children's nurses and the laundress, whose work looking after the household linen must have been very arduous, but who was one of the lowest-paid workers in the castle. The highest-paid servant was the one whose job it was to clean out the latrines. There were usually latrines (garderobes or privies) built into the walls on each floor of the keep. They emptied into the moat, or simply outside the wall, or, in the case of those at Tintagel Castle, over the cliff. There was a garderobe shaft serving the top end of the great hall at Launceston. The accumulated waste needed to be buried at frequent intervals. If the castle was under siege and this could not be done, the waste bred fevers and often the defenders were obliged to surrender the keep because they were weakened by illness. Chamber pots do appear in household accounts.

Most of the domestic work of the castle was performed by men, as it was of necessity on a large scale, using the heaviest of utensils. Cooking was often done in the open air or in a separate outdoor kitchen because of the constant danger of fire. In the women's apartments no doubt a good deal of cooking was done in the fireplace, for children or for any small meals. Cauldrons have changed little in design over hundreds of years. They were hung on an iron hanger of a type that has been in use until the present century. A kitchen at Launceston was built in stone in the mid-thirteenth century against the bailey rampart, serving the great hall. It was a square building with walls one metre thick, originally with a central fire, which may have had a louvre or hood over it, through which the heat and smoke could escape and which kept the rain out. The heat was often so great that many of the cooks can be seen in illustrations of the time working naked, using old archery targets as fire screens.

Castle kitchens usually had an enormous chopping block and a large pestle and mortar for pounding food and herbs. These would have been well used, as most medieval recipes start with the instruction to the cook to 'smite him to pecys'.

The kitchen at Launceston later became a brew and bakehouse. In all castles constant changes took place throughout their history. Launceston being the county town until the nineteenth century, its castle remained important enough to have many improvements made over the years. Those undertaken by Earl Richard in the mid-thirteenth century included the building of the strong cylindrical stone tower in the middle of the earlier shell keep, rising well above the outer wall. This is approached by a stone staircase up the side of the mound, defended at the bottom by a gatehouse. A shell keep has a stone ring wall crowning the mound and can be seen in the best-preserved and finest unaltered example of a Cornish castle at Trematon, near Saltash. This was gradually refortified in the thirteenth century, when the bailey was surrounded by a curtain wall with a three-storey gatehouse. This wall was pulled down in the nineteenth century when the present house was built inside the bailey.

Another shell keep at the castle of Restormel, near Lostwithiel, is all that remains of what was one of the most beautiful of Cornish castles. It was sold to Earl Richard by Isolda de Cardinan of the wealthy Cardinham family in 1268. He already owned Launceston and Tintagel and had forced the owner of Trematon Castle to sell that to him as well. Many Norman noblemen owned several castles and spent their time travelling from one to the other, along with their retinues, taking all their furnishings and possessions with them, down to and including the tapestries on their walls. This was obviously safer than leaving them behind in those days.

When Earl Richard died in 1272, the keep was converted by his son, Edmund, into a residential tower with private domestic accommodation two storeys high round a central courtyard, containing its own hall and great kitchen, the latter rising to the full height of the building. The circle of rooms also included a chapel, a solar and bedchambers. The hall and solar were well lit with large windows and warmed by fireplaces. All parts of the keep were supplied with a plentiful supply of fresh water. All this was in addition to the buildings in the bailey, which included a further hall, chambers, chapel and kitchen, probably for the use of the retainers. The whole castle was set in its own deer park, the largest in the duchy, providing hunting for the earl. There was a substantial fishery in the nearby River Fowey.

The diet of a Norman baron was usually supplemented with venison and game from hunting, an activity no longer allowed to the poor as it had been in Saxon times. Hunting in his own forest was now strictly the lord's prerogative and anyone poaching on his preserves risked death or maiming. Lesser mortals might be lucky enough to be given the hearts, liver and entrails of the deer, known as 'umbles', to be made into umble pie.

Richard I had begun the practice of selling immunity from forest laws to such of his subjects willing to pay for this. In 1204 Cornwall was prepared to pay as much as 2,200 marks for the disafforestation of the whole of the county. Such was the importance to Celtic Cornwall of the right to hunt in their own forests.

With these amenities, Restormel became a favourite castle of Edward, the Black Prince, and his knights in the fourteenth century, and he paid more than one visit to the duchy. He was created the first Duke of Cornwall in 1337 by his father, Edward III, and became Prince of Wales in 1343. One of his visits in 1363 lasted for three months. An expedition to Gascony was being prepared at Plymouth and he needed to raise men for the venture. After his death the Dukes of Cornwall never visited their castles again. They began to fall into disrepair, in spite of repeated requests from the duchy to the King and Parliament for them to be repaired and manned, especially when France and Spain were later threatening the Cornish coasts. The deer parks were turned into pasture in the reign of Henry VIII. By the time of Elizabeth I, the historian John Norden wrote that Restormel Castle 'beginneth to mourne and to wringe out hard stones for tears; she that was embraced, visited and delighted with great princes, is now desolate, forsaken and forlorne'. In the Civil War the government forces reported that Restormel was 'utterly ruined, nothing but the outer walls thereof remaining, which are not worth taking down'.

The castles that were built by Henry VIII along the south coast were military fortresses against a possible French invasion. Those at Pendennis and St Mawes were paid for out of money obtained from the dissolution of the monasteries. They are solid gun emplacements showing the established supremacy of gunpowder by this time. Castles were now out of private hands and owned by the King.

If Launceston Castle was terrible, Trematon Castle enduring and Restormel romantic, Tintagel Castle, of which one has the greatest hopes because of its reputed association with the birth of King Arthur, turns out to be a disappointment at first, when its date long after his birth is realized. Its beauty and the grandeur of its position on the cliffs are undeniable, but seeing it through the often-present mists of the north Cornwall coast has confused the minds of many, and made sorting out the myths from reality not easy.

As Duke of Cornwall, the Black Prince owned Tintagel in the fourteenth century but, after his death, the castle slowly decayed. It was repaired and used as a prison at the end of that century.

If Restormel Castle was desolate, forsaken and forlorn at the end of its most glorious years, no one can think this of Tintagel. It is now overwhelmed with visitors, perhaps still hoping to find King Arthur and the sixth-century magic that still surrounds his name, and hoping that the Celtic myths will be proved true.

CHAPTER 7

Fear and Strife

I N THE fourteenth and fifteenth centuries the well-established homes of the most famous families of Cornwall, as well as the homes of the majority of the ordinary people of the county, were undermined by new fears, over and above the continuing worries they had always endured. They had always coped with litigation and property disputes with their neighbours, and even enjoyed them. They took part in wars and political disputes when necessary, as far as they affected their homes and their county. Now the atmosphere changed. More and more, the Cornish were drawn into events happening outside their homes, their county and their country.

The religious difficulties and differences that surfaced in Tudor times invaded the homes of both rich and poor. Religious beliefs, ever close to Celtic hearts, tore apart families that had once always supported each other in true Celtic fashion. Now they were divided as they had not been before.

The manor houses of Cornwall had been comparatively peaceful places in earlier centuries. From manorial records we can see that they were run in an orderly way and were of necessity both self-sufficient and efficient. Many families were related by marriage and were constant visitors to each others' homes. Richard Carew, in his sixteenth century *Survey of Cornwall*, said that all Cornish gentlemen were cousins and constantly visited each other. 'A gentleman and his wife will ride to make merry with his neighbour and after a day or twayne these two couples go to a third, in which progress they increase like snowballs till through their burdensome weight they break again'.

The constant visiting between the Arundells of Trerice, the Arundells of Lanherne, the Carews of Antony and the Grenvilles of Stowe, among others, is more remarkable when one considers the state of the roads and the fact that the journeys were made on horseback, ladies riding on pillions behind their servants, or in litters carried between two horses. Carriages were rare and those that existed were more like farm carts, needing several horses to pull them over the rough roads, through fords and mud. There must have been a strong Celtic desire for feasting and fun for them to suffer all this.

Entertaining in a manor house where visitors were to stay overnight cannot have been easy. These were not grand stately homes of wealthy noble families – there were few of these in Cornwall. They were reasonably sized working houses, to a great extent self-supporting, where often the lady of the manor alone was responsible for providing all food, furnishings and clothing for the long medieval winter, unless the lord of the manor had a steward who attended to some of these matters.

Many manors in the early Middle Ages were still little more than the one-roomed halls of the Anglo-Saxons, although in time extra rooms may have been added, as well as domestic quarters for the servants.

A good example of how small a Cornish manor house could be is the Old Post Office at Tintagel, originally a fourteenth-century manor house. Built low to withstand the weather of the north coast, it has walls 750 millimetres to one metre thick of local stone and slate. The rafters have bent under the great weight of the slate roof, giving the uneven and picturesque appearance it has today. Slate was also used when the fireplace was built into the wall of the hall, open to the rafters above. These are blackened by the smoke from the fires originally in the centre of the floor. The large slate overmantel of the fifteenth-century fireplace is some 2.5 metres long and 1.25 metres high, supported by slate jambs on either side. This hall would have been the centre of life in the home, where the family lived and slept with their servants, cosy but crowded. The house is entered by an outside porch, giving it added protection from the weather, leading into 'the entry', a passage that ran through many Cornish homes from the front to the back entrance, with the hall on one side and the parlour on the other. Both these rooms have wall ovens at the side of their hearths, showing the multi-purpose uses of medieval rooms. There is a spiral stone staircase in a semicircular turret in one corner of the hall leading to a bedchamber above. A bedroom over the parlour is reached by another steep and narrow staircase.

The house has been through many changes, but is still standing on

Window in Tintagel Old Post Office

the site it occupied in the fourteenth century. It was once the village post office, and at the far side of the hall is the entrance to a small room, now furnished as a Victorian village post office by the National Trust, which today owns the building. The rooms are dark, lit with tiny slit windows, some hewn out of a single piece of local greenstone. All the materials used would have been local, owing to the difficulties and cost of transport. The large slate quarry at Delabole is not far away.

Many of the homes of the most famous Cornish families of the Middle Ages have now disappeared, leaving only traces of their former existence – a wall here, a tower there, or an impressive gateway now leading only to an open field. While some are now farmhouses, some even only barns, many have been adapted as comfortable modern homes. Others are today among the best-known and best-loved of Cornish houses 'open to the public', such as Cotehele and Trerice.

The manor of Berry Court, Penhallam, Jacobstow, had fine stone buildings around a courtyard, with a ground-floor hall, still with a central fire. The buildings were of twelfth-to fourteenth-century date, and the whole was surrounded by a moat crossed by a drawbridge. There was a chapel and domestic quarters with a kitchen, buttery, bake and brewhouses and a pantry. This type of home illustrated the transition from the castle to the simple undefended manor house.

Few of these manors betray their often turbulent past, when a knock at the door could mean a search for a hole where a priest might be hiding. A wife alone might find foreign raiders at her door, forcing her to defend her home as best she could without her husband's help. She had to be prepared to cope when he was away at war, or in court in London defending his right to his land or, more often than not, in prison if he had been unsuccessful in any of these exploits. In medieval times, when their lords went to war, many of their retainers had to follow them, perhaps to Agincourt or Crécy, further depleting any male help available at home.

Even later, in 1457, Place, the undefended home of Thomas Treffy in Fowey, had to be defended by his wife when he was absent and the town was attacked by the Breton fleet. The surprised inhabitants sheltered in her home. No doubt she more than encouraged her husband when he decided to turn his house into a fortified manor on his return.

As early as the fourteenth century Cornish ports had been called upon to supply ships to repel French raiders along the south coast of Cornwall. Seventy Cornish ships helped to gain control of the Channel by 1340.

Cornwall again made a large contribution to the fleet that sailed to France in 1346 under Edward III, who took with him a young Duke of Cornwall, now Prince of Wales. This expedition ended in the English capturing Calais, a possession held by the English crown for the next two centuries.

Two years later Cornwall was hit, like the rest of the country, by the Black Death. It suffered a little less than other counties, because there were not so many large towns where overcrowded conditions encouraged the greatest spread of infection. Towns like Bodmin, where sanitary arrangements were sparse, were affected the most – only two of the canons in the priory there were spared. The tin mines were badly affected with the loss of many working tinners, and only at the end of the century did things improve, when an increase in workers brought the mines back to prosperity.

The manors were also to suffer from a shortage of labour on the land. Sheep farming requiring little labour took the place of crop production. By the fifteenth century the owners of the manors were looking for other means of acquiring income from their estates.

Cornish ships again benefited from the continuing war with France which increased trade and a demand for Cornish tin. A new class of Cornish yeoman farmers and merchants was arising.

While Cornwall was flourishing, the events outside the county were increasingly deteriorating. The visits of the Black Prince to his duchy in 1354 and 1356, after victories against the French, were followed by disasters after his death and that of his father. Most of their French possessions were lost, and the Cornish castles were neglected and were mostly in ruins. To add to the troubles of Cornwall both the French and Spanish were raiding the southern coast again, killing and burning, leading the Cornish to complain that they couldn't defend their own coast as so many of their men had been impressed into the navy.

Cornish discontent at the time of the Peasants' Revolt in 1381 was mainly directed against the clergy, some of whom met untimely ends at the hands of irate parishioners. When peace with France came, and pilgrimages to such place as the shrine of St James at Compostela began again, the atmosphere became calmer. The pilgrims from Ireland and Wales travelled to Padstow and on by the well-worn route to Fowey via St Michael's Mount, then by Cornish ships to France.

The French and English were still accusing each other of acts of piracy. Nineteen Cornish fishing boats were sunk at Looe in 1405 by French and Spanish vessels which burned and sacked the town.

Cornish ships were again in the fleet that sailed to France with Henry V in 1415, leading to eventual victory at Agincourt, where the Cornishmen fought under a banner showing two wrestlers. The King later invited them to attend a sporting festival. As in the past, the

Cornish contribution was mainly in transporting troops and supplies, manning their vessels in war and in peace to travel the seas with which they were so familiar. When not so concerned with war, the seamen of Cornwall occupied themselves with acts of piracy, particularly those sailing out of Fowey.

Acts of piracy along the Cornish coasts and those of Brittany continued unabated at this time, but at a generally accepted level. The Cornish, at heart, were always ready to leave for other countries by sea, but as they showed in the next century, they were not anxious to cross the border to England to fight on land. Sufficiently roused, however, by threats to their livelihood or their homes, they were always willing to follow a leader to remedy the situation. When in 1497 Parliament voted for heavy taxation to pay for Henry VII's Scottish war, the minds of Cornishmen were turned to matters beyond their own coastline, and they made their first incursion into England. The revolt against the taxes originated in the Lizard peninsula. At first it was led by a blacksmith, Michael Joseph of St Keverne, but it soon spread throughout the county as far as Bodmin. Here their spokesman was a lawyer named Thomas Flamank, who persuaded them that the law was on their side and that money could not be raised for a Scottish war. The protesters marched into Devon and Somerset, collecting supporters along the way. They continued through Wiltshire and Surrey and almost reached Kent; they then turned towards London.

The army of ten thousand that the King had prepared for Scotland was turned to defend the city against the Cornish, who fought bravely in the ensuing battle at Blackheath against overwhelming odds. The battle was lost before it had begun.

This had been the first time the Cornish had ventured into England in such numbers, and this experience would not encourage them to do it again for some time. About two hundred Cornishmen were killed at Blackheath. The leaders were hanged, drawn and quartered at Tyburn. Lord Audley, who had taken over command at Wells, was beheaded at Tower Hill. The King later pardoned all offenders who submitted to his mercy, but the Cornish were unrepentant after their failure.

The rebellious Cornish mood was further strengthened by the arrival at Whitesand Bay, near Land's End, of Perkin Warbeck, claiming to be the rightful King of England. He had 120 followers with him and was given a rapturous reception when he raised his standard at Penzance. He professed to be the younger of the two princes murdered in the Tower by Richard III, and therefore to be Richard, Duke of York. He had come via Ireland on hearing of the march of the Cornish on London, in the hope of finding support from them while they were in a rebellious mood. He had the support of the King of Scotland, and had married Lady Catherine Gordon, a near relative of the King. He left his beautiful wife in the care of the monks at St Michael's Mount while he proceeded to Bodmin, where he was proclaimed King Richard IV.

By the time Warbeck crossed the Tamar into Devon he had acquired a force of six thousand men, with which he laid siege to Exeter, only to find that the city had been reinforced by the Earl of Devon and his forces. Once again, after fierce fighting, the Cornish suffered defeat. Reaching Taunton, with the King's forces approaching, Warbeck deserted his troops and took sanctuary in Beaulieu Abbey, near Southampton. He surrendered to the King's mercy. When the King arrived, he sent for Lady Catherine, and was so impressed with her beauty that she was sent to the Queen at the court in London. Warbeck was kept at court as well, but was hanged two years later for his part in another conspiracy. Henry pardoned most of the Cornish rebels, although a few of their leaders were executed, but he sent tax collectors to levy heavy taxes on Cornwall, which was a very great burden on the impoverished county and a severe punishment.

This low point in Cornish fortunes was soon followed by the dissolution of the monasteries. The little Benedictine priory of Tywardreath was one of the first to go, but the priory at St Michael's Mount was saved and strengthened as an important military and economic site. The fate of the monasteries was followed by the surrender of the friaries, first Bodmin, then Truro. The religious profile of Cornwall that had prevailed since the fourth century was changed forever.

From the time of the dissolution of the monasteries under Henry VIII, many of the gentry and middle classes ascended the social scale, acquiring lands and property that has formerly been in the hands of the Church, often as a reward for helping the King.

Nicholas Prideaux acquired the tithes and lands of a number of parishes for his help with the work of dissolution. These included the area of Padstow, formerly owned by Bodmin Priory, where his family were to build Place, a splendid Elizabethan house overlooking the estuary. The original building was in the traditional E shape, still discernible on its eastern front, but additions and alterations of the eighteenth and nineteenth centuries gave the original manor house the more Gothic appearance it has today.

Many of these new owners were able to exploit the mineral resources of their newly acquired land. One such was Sir William Godolphin, whose tin works became the largest in Cornwall at this time. He built Godolphin Hall, a house much extended in the seventeenth century, when the family rose to even greater power. Some of the money came from the tin mines and some from the rights to the royalties from wrecks, a bonus enjoyed by many owners whose properties adjoined the coasts. Many valuables from the wrecks found their way into their homes.

Cotehele, ('the wood by the estuary') on the west bank of the Tamar, on the boundary between Devon and Cornwall, was a small manor

The manor house at Cotehele

house in the reign of Edward III, when Hilaria de Cotehele brought it to her husband, William Edgecumbe, on her marriage in 1353. For the next two hundred years, the Edgcumbes lived there, extending their house and land through inheritance and the women they married, as was usual in the Middle Ages. Land was the only real wealth and was fought for both physically and in the courts of law.

In 1483 Cotehele was surrounded by the forces of Sir Henry Trenowth of Bodrugan, an agent of Richard III. The then owner, Richard Edgcumbe, had sided against the King after hearing rumours that he had murdered the two little princes, the sons of Edward IV, in the Tower of London. Perhaps he thought he was safe in secluded Cotehele, so far from the scene of the crime, but he was forced to flee from his enemies down the river, cutting the throat of a sentry and fooling his pursuers by throwing his cap into the water. Leaving them to think he had drowned, he escaped to Brittany, where he joined forces with Henry Tudor. He fought successfully with him at the Battle of Bosworth in 1485 and was knighted for his efforts, returning home at last when peace was restored to build the small chapel in the wood at Cotehele in grateful thanks for his safe delivery. Such changes in the fortunes of a manor owner were not unusual. Most can only rarely have been in residence. Edgcumbe travelled extensively for the King, only supervising the alterations and extensions to Cotehele during brief visits there, eventually dying abroad, the fate of so many Cornishmen.

Richard Edgcumbe made the alterations and additions to his home in the last years of his life, in keeping with his exalted position. He built the imposing entrance tower and south front, as well as extra accommodation around the inner court and the chapel. This replaced an earlier chapel – even in small manors a chapel was of premier importance in the lives of the inhabitants. Although the Wars of the Roses were over and most houses built at this time concentrated on providing more comfort and light, with windows looking out on a slightly more peaceful world, Edgcumbe continued to fit his house with battlements on the tower, small windows and easily defended gateways. His experiences of 1483 were obviously still on his mind.

The work was continued by his son Piers, who completed the hall range by 1520, being similarly conservative and cautious about introducing new ideas. Most hall houses being built then were made a little less draughty by a screened passage at one end of the hall, together with an entrance porch, to protect the occupants from the worst of the draughts. Piers's hall has no passage, porch or screen of any kind, being entered directly from the hall court.

Originally the family would have sat on a raised dais at the end of the hall furthest from the entrance, where there was a large fireplace to keep them warm. In time they migrated from here to the old dining room at the side of the hall, eventually reaching the new dining room in the east wing in the nineteenth century. Both these rooms took them further away from the kitchen which had been near the hall, so hot meals and convenience were gradually sacrificed to privacy and perhaps warmth. The ancient Celts would never have approved of this. However, the kitchen at Cotehele was well equipped. There were pot hooks with adjustable hangers to hold kettles and cauldrons in the kitchen hearth. The kettle has a 'handy maid' device that can tip a kettle or pot forward and reduce the effort of lifting heavy utensils when pouring liquids. In place of a modern thermostat, there are hooks at various heights to control the heat under the cauldron by raising or lowering it.

Although, for the most part, the hot and heavy work, in medieval kitchens was done by men, these improvements in the kitchen at Cotehele do suggest that women were supervising the meals here and that, as time passed, they had talked the estate blacksmith into making life a little easier for them. Medieval kitchens were often built outside timber-framed houses, but at Cotehele, where the buildings were of stone and granite, reducing the danger of fire, the kitchen was an integral part of the house.

The solar or private living room of the family was built above the old dining room and has two squint holes, one so the lady of the manor could see what was happening in the hall below and one looking down on the chapel. It seems that the household was a fairly orderly one. The oldest clock in England, installed by Sir Richard, is still in its original position in the chapel, although not now in use. It controlled two bells, one calling the household to Mass and one striking the hours. There would have been a resident priest with considerable influence over the household, probably also acting as secretary to the lord of the manor.

The manor court and much official business would have been conducted in the hall, particularly when the family moved to other rooms.

Cotehele has been little changed over the centuries, principally
because, instead of altering the house as did so many of his friends
during the great rebuilding that went on in the sixteenth century, a later
Sir Richard Edgcumbe built a new family seat at Mount Edgcumbe,
again by the water, and thereafter Cotehele was kept mainly as a home
for older family members, with little alteration to the house or its furnishings. The plain medieval walls are still covered with tapestries, not
so much for decoration as for warmth, cut to fit round doors and
windows like wallpaper.

Of Richard Carew's home at Antony, little can now be seen. He was
born there in 1555, but the house that can be seen there today was built
in 1721 and is one of the best examples of an eighteenth-century
Cornish house. Carew built a saltwater pond on the shore of his estate,
which became one of the great interests of his life, a retreat where he
could go alone or with a friend in the evening to watch the fish coming
to be fed at the sound of their food being chopped. A well-read country
gentleman with many interests, his *Survey of Cornwall*, published in 1602,
gives us the most complete picture of Cornwall in his lifetime that we
have. In it he tells of one of the difficulties with which he had to
contend while writing it. 'Of all manner of vermin, Cornish houses are
most pestered with rats, a brood very hurtful for devouring of meat,
clothes and writings by day, and alike cumbersome through their crying
and rattling, while they dance their gallop gallyards in the roof at night.'

The Arundell family, with whom Carew was closely connected in
friendship and marriage, was the best-known and best-loved family in
Cornwall, known by the country people as 'the great Arundells'. One
branch of the family lived at Lanherne, St Mawgan, and remained
staunch Catholics throughout the Reformation; the other branch lived
at Trerice, near Newquay, rebuilt in about 1570 by Sir John Arundell.
They first acquired the property by marriage in the reign of Edward III,
and they remained there for the next four hundred years.

Trerice is a more compact house than Cotehele, entered through a
porch and screened passage, with the kitchens on one side and the hall
on the other. The hall rises through two floors and has some fine plas-

Chi verace ducera   *Ann° dm̄. 1586*

Ætatis suæ 32.

Richard Carew of Antony

terwork on the ceiling, incorporating the initials J.A, K.A and M.A, of Sir John, his wife Katherine and his sister Margaret. It is possible that to make the hall even cosier, it had a carved screen at the entrance and wainscoting around the walls, long since removed. It has a less medieval look than the hall built fifty years earlier at Cotehele. It certainly let in more light – the great hall window had twenty-four lights and 576

Trerice, the hall with its plaster ceiling and the musicians gallery.

panes, many of which still have the original sixteenth-century glass. Few windows had glass before Tudor times, making do with panes of horn or linen dipped in wax. The large fireplace and overmantel with the date 1572, in the middle of the wall opposite, give the impression of a comfortable Elizabethan home looking out on the world with confidence, rather than the fortified, inward-looking homes of the past. With background music provided from the musicians' gallery at the far end of the hall, the house must have been a pleasant place to visit then, as it is today. 'Tre' is the Cornish prefix for a homestead, and as Carew says, 'res signifieth a rushing or floating away, and on the declining of a hill the house is seated'.

The solar of the house at Trerice is now known as the drawing room and probably always fulfilled that purpose. It has an even more elaborate ceiling and fireplace than the hall, although the plasterer ran out of space when carving the date in grand style, right across the top of the overmantel, ANNO:DOMINI:MCCCCCLXX3, the 3 added when there was no room for III. In spite of this the plasterwork is without doubt the work of a master craftsman, whose art can be seen in several Cornish houses of the time, perhaps recommended by one owner to another on their frequent mutual visits.

In the middle of the sixteenth century the changes in the Church that had begun with the Reformation slowly became apparent to those attending their parish churches. As the monasteries disappeared there was an increase in the building of these parish churches, which the Cornish grew to love, as much as they loved the services that took place in them. Arguments were brought to a head by the issue of the first edition of Archibishop Cranmer's Prayer Book, and an Act of Uniformity passed to enforce its use. This brought the differences between Catholic and Protestant into the open. But only in the extreme south-west did open rebellion to the changes take place. The Cornish Celts, who had disliked the Church of Rome centuries before, had now become very attached to their version of it, even if the Mass was in Latin and not Cornish. Now they resented having a service in English forced on them, and having the festivals they loved disallowed: no candles, no ashes, no images in the church, no palms on Palm Sunday. This upset them more than the dissolution of the monasteries had done.

Most of the Cornish still spoke their old Cornish Celtic language, but preferred the Latin Mass to the English version, which they called the 'Christmas play'. The opportunity to preserve the Cornish language was lost, and it was destined to disappear as the people of Cornwall gradually came to accept the use of English.

Once more St Keverne in the Lizard peninsula, where the rebellion against taxation in 1497 was led by blacksmith Michael Joseph, was again involved in turmoil. The priest there, Martin Geoffrey, together with William and John Kilter of Constantine, led a thousand men to attack one William Body, who was overseeing the destruction of the images in Helston Church. They stabbed him to death. This revolt was soon crushed, only to rise again the next year, 1549, when the Act of Uniformity was passed. The rebels demanded that the Latin Mass be restored. They were led by two Catholic landowners, Humphry Arundell and John Winslade. The former was the Governor of St Michael's Mount, but was not present when the rebellion began. A number of families sought protection from the rebels in the mount, but were forced to surrender when a smokescreen made by trusses of burning hay, a shortage of food and the cries of the distressed women made further resistance impossible. They were taken to the headquarters of the rebels in Bodmin. Once again, after fierce fighting, they were defeated near Exeter, after a five-week siege of the town. Humphry Arundell and Winslade, with two of their Devonshire companions, were eventually hanged at Tyburn.

Under Queen Elizabeth the prosperity of all the great families of Cornwall was initially assured, and it was also a time of comparative toleration of their beliefs. But from the time she was excommunicated in 1570, all her subjects had to choose between loyalty to their queen or loyalty to the Pope. At Trerice they sided with the Queen and later in the Civil War fought with the royalists. But at nearby Lanherne, the Arundell family remained staunch Catholics throughout the Reformation. At the beginning of the sixteenth century, John Arundell became Dean of Exeter, Bishop of Lichfield and Coventry, and then Bishop of Exeter. He continued the generous hospitality that had been a mark of Lanherne at Exeter, with a daily distribution of alms at his palace gate. It is claimed that Mass has been said at Lanherne without a break until the present day, since the house was inhabited by the nuns who came there in 1794 and founded their Carmelite convent. It is situated in one of the most beautiful and peaceful valleys in Cornwall, separated by a wall from the nearby Protestant church of St Mawgan, where there are several brasses in memory of the Arundell family. The house kept its Elizabethan front when it was altered and added to in the seventeenth and eighteenth centuries.

Only the most wealthy Catholics could afford the fines for not conforming and attending the new services, and many suffered imprisonment. Even the 'great Arundells' were eventually impoverished by the persecution. They were closely linked in friendship, marriage and religion with the Tregian family of Golden, a Tudor house overlooking the valley of the Upper Fal, near Grampound, Tregony, now a farm with a large buttressed stone barn, which may have been the original manor house. It was here that Francis Tregian harboured the priest Cuthbert Mayne, who held forbidden services, both at Lanherne and Golden, passing as Tregian's steward.

Cuthbert Mayne was born near Barnstaple in Devon in 1544. His family were happy to follow the new form of Anglican service, and until he went to Oxford University in 1567, he found no difficulty in serving the reformed English Church. But the changes were to be increasingly severely enforced as the years went by.

At Oxford he made friends with many of the young men who were becoming deeply disturbed at having to make definite decisions as to where their loyalties lay. They had been discussing and arguing religious questions, as students do. But the time came when it was not possible to go to Mass in secret while attending services following the Anglican rites in public, as many of them had been doing. Gradually the situation became more difficult, and the Church had its spies in the colleges. What had been purely academic problems became major issues. One by one students left their studies and the life in Oxford that they loved, and returned to their homes, or left for the new training college for priests in France, in the hope of avoiding becoming involved in the religious conflict. This was the path that Cuthbert Mayne was to follow. His great influence and friend at college was Edmund Campion, who was fast coming to the conclusion that to go ahead with ordination into the Anglican Church, as had been the hope of most of the scholars, was wrong, and that the Catholic Church was the only way to salvation. In 1569 Campion left Oxford and went to Ireland. Cuthbert Mayne soon followed his example and went home to Devon. He then set in motion the preliminaries that would at last admit him to Douai. This was the training ground of the missionary priests whose aim was the restoration of the Mass and the Catholic Church in England. He spent three years wrestling with his decision, meanwhile moving to Cornwall, learning all the time of the lives and hopes of the Catholic families there. From Cornwall he journeyed to Douai, where he renewed his acquaintance with Campion, eventually to follow him into martyrdom. Mayne was later to be ordained a priest there and to return to his native land, a suspect and prohibited person.

In Cornwall he found unease in family loyalties and religious differences among the gentry. Intermarriage between these families made the differences more difficult. In 1576 Mayne took up a post at Golden Manor as steward to Francis Tregian, a devout Catholic, who had longed for a priest to administer the faith to his family and friends. A system of communication was devised whereby when the priest was able to say the forbidden Mass the news could be passed to nearby Catholics. To attend Mass amounted to treason, but there were many willing to risk this. Mayne travelled to Lanherne and other houses in the area to say Mass, children were baptized, marriages were regularized, and the sacraments administered. Unchallenged for the time being in this remote corner of the county, he ventured further afield, as far as Launceston.

In June 1577 the situation changed abruptly. Richard Grenville, Sheriff of Cornwall, a strong anti-Catholic, acting on information that the Mass was being said there, entered Golden on the pretext of searching for an escaped prisoner. On meeting Cuthbert Mayne he discovered the little wax emblem round his neck, the sign of the Lamb of God, the Agnus Dei. On further searching, papers and letters, rosary beads and the priest's stole were found and confiscated. The papers included what the prosecution would say was a copy of the Bull of Excommunication of the Queen, evidence enough of the priest's involvement for a conviction of treason and a sentence of death. He was arrested along with Francis Tregian. The latter was later allowed to return to his family, having paid a large sum of money as surety for good behaviour and confirmation that he would appear at the autumn assize in Launceston. The priest, however, was to receive very different treatment. He was to spend months in the dungeon of Launceston Castle, while many other Catholics in the area were rounded up for questioning.

The long-drawn-out trial of the priest and those other Catholics said to be involved with him proceeded to its inevitable end. Richard Grenville sought to involve as many as he could in the trial of the simple priest and the man whose steward he was, and he succeeded in his objective. Cuthbert Mayne was pronounced guilty of high treason, and St Andrew's Day, 30 November 1577, was named as the day of execution. He was hanged, drawn and quartered on the appointed day, his head being impaled on the gate of Launceston Castle. The four quarters of his body were to be exposed at Barnstaple, Bodmin, Wadebridge and Tregony for all to see. The sheriff broke into Tregian's home at Golden at night and evicted his wife and family. Tregian was thrown into the dreaded dungeon of Launceston Castle. After spending eighteen years in various prisons, he was allowed to travel abroad and died in Lisbon in 1608. He received a pension from the King of Spain for his devotion to his faith, while Grenville was knighted for his services to his queen.

While there are several priest's holes at Lanherne, Sir John Arundell was eventually imprisoned in the Tower of London for harbouring priests in his London home. Later he was less rigorously confined and he died in Isleworth in 1590, his body being returned to St Columb for burial. It must have been a sad time at Lanherne during these years when the family was at odds with the Arundells of Trerice, a far cry from a hundred years or so earlier, when items for the Christmas celebrations in the Lanherne accounts included paper and holland cloth for decorations and four dozen bells for the Morris dancers.

The family of Richard Grenville had lived at Stowe, near Kilkhampton, throughout the Middle Ages, increasing their wealth and property by marrying into several famous families of the time, including the Arundells and the Courtenays of Powderham, who later became the Earls of Devon. A Thomas Grenville and the Courtenays had been involved with Richard Edgcumbe in the plot against Richard III. The Grenvilles were one of the rising families on the seesaw of power in the late sixteenth century, when the Arundells were descending. Richard Grenville's father had gone down with the *Mary Rose*, King Henry VIII's flagship, of which he was captain, when it sank in the Solent in 1545. The ship was to be raised in 1984 to provide much information on the life of the Tudor sailors. Richard was born in 1542, about the same time as Sir Francis Drake, and was one of the number of West Country sailors whose names have gone down in history. Along with Godolphin and John Arundell of Trerice, he organized the defence of Cornwall when the Armada threatened, returning to his home at Stowe to await its approach, as did Cornishmen all around the coast. They waited and watched, with arms and harness at the ready, until the Armada had passed by to its defeat further up the Channel. Grenville was one of the founders of the Virginia colony in America and was to die engaging some fifteen Spanish vessels off Flores in the Azores in Drake's ship, the *Revenge*, an exploit later commemorated in the famous poem by Tennyson.

Trerice, Cotehele and Lanherne are each flourishing in their own way today, although the families that lived in them have gone, while the home of the Grenvilles at Stowe has long since vanished.

In October 1970, when all the English bishops assembled in Rome to take part in the canonization of Cuthbert Mayne, the Pope read out the list of the Forty Martyrs who had suffered for their faith. Cuthbert Mayne's name was the first, because he had been the first of the seminary priests to give his life in testimony of the Christian faith. Cornwall had its first truly canonized saint.

CHAPTER 8

War and Warriors

THE SEVENTEENTH CENTURY brought out all that was best in the Celtic character of the Cornish – the love they had for their families, their homes and their county, their love of justice and freedom of thought, and their religious fervour, whatever their beliefs and whichever side of a contest they supported. Together with their courage and their great loyalty to their leaders, these qualities were to be enhanced by the events that put the Cornish, for the first time in their history, at the forefront of what was happening in the nation as a whole.

Men felt more secure than in the past and put their confidence in the future into the renovation and enlargement of their homes. It was the great age of rebuilding which had started in the Elizabethan period. Many had acquired new homes and land when the monasteries were dissolved. The owners of manor houses were now free from the feudal and religious restrictions of the Middle Ages. Yeoman farmers were prospering from ever-increasing markets for their produce. There was a demand for more comfort in the home and a greater variety of goods to fill the extra rooms that were added to the new houses. The occupants now viewed the world through large glazed windows facing outward instead of inward into secluded courtyards.

There was, however, still the problem of Spain. Not only were the Cornish ports in a vulnerable position if Spain should invade, but the tin industry was under great pressure to increase its production to assist preparations for defence. It needed capitalist help to dig deeper for the tin that was there but underground. No longer were the streams of Cornwall able to supply enough within easy reach. But to dig deeper required equipment and therefore money. Luckily the gentry who had acquired new homes and additional land after the dissolution were only too eager to accrue wealth by exploiting the minerals they now owned.

One of the foremost mine-owners was Sir Francis Godolphin,

whose tin works near Helston were the largest in Cornwall. He was able to employ skilled German mining engineers and three hundred workers. With the threat of invasion ever present, preparations for the defence of the county went ahead.

The Lieutenant-General of Cornwall and Lord Warden of the Stannaries, Sir Walter Raleigh, together with his deputy lieutenants, organized training for tinners and workers on the land for the militia. The Iron Age hill forts of Cornwall came into use again, with beacons manned at the highest points ready to warn of enemy approach.

The Spanish sailed past the Cornish coast in 1588 and were defeated further up the Channel by the English fleet. They sailed past Mount Edgcumbe, the home of the Edgcumbe family. It was said that their commander, the Duke of Medina Sidonia, had marked out the house for himself when he had succeeded in conquering England. The Queen had hoped to deal with the situation by small encounters with the Spanish as her sailors searched for Spanish treasure. The danger to Cornwall became even greater when the Spanish occupied Brittany in 1590. Sir Richard Grenville took part in an encounter in the Azores in 1591, when he alone engaged fifty-three opponents in his ship *Revenge,* fighting his last heroic action to the death.

St Michael's Mount Bay became the scene of much activity in 1595. The Spanish burnt Mousehole and the churches at Paul, Newlyn and Penzance. By the time Sir Francis Drake came to the aid of Sir Francis Godolphin during this encounter, changes in wind and weather helped the Spanish to escape. The winds that so often lashed the Cornish coasts, making life difficult for their fishermen, often came to their aid, blowing their enemies away.

Elizabeth, realizing that the situation was deteriorating, sent for Drake, who with Hawkins was to raid the Spanish Main, but both the commanders were killed in the operation. There was no shortage in Cornwall of valiant sailors willing to come to the aid of England, and soon the Earl of Essex and Sir Walter Raleigh captured Cadiz and further damaged the Armada. The government realized that Cornwall and its ships could not go on repelling the Spaniards alone and sent soldiers to reinforce Plymouth and Pendennis Castle. When the Armada sailed again, in spite of all the preparations that were now in place for the defence of Cornwall, it was once more the weather which proved the greatest help in defeating it. The fierce gales in the Channel in the autumn of 1597 drove the Spanish once more from English shores.

Elizabeth left the country in a fairly peaceful and prosperous state at the end of her life. There had been no eldest son of the monarch to be Duke of Cornwall during her reign. The gentry had been the leaders of the Cornish during this time, as they were also to be in the century to come. When James I became King in 1603, Cornwall again had a Duke. By this time the duchy was much reduced, as Elizabeth in her money-raising efforts in the last years of her reign, had sold eighteen of its manors, although not entitled to do so. These included Trematon, Tintagel and Restormel. James, to his credit, invoked the power of Parliament and recovered them for his son Henry.

The new reign began with a welcome end to the Spanish war, but now leaving the Cornish coast to be attacked by pirates from Algiers and Morocco. In 1625 these pirates took twenty-seven ships and 200 men, eighty from Looe, and sixty men, women and children snatched from a church near Mount's Bay. Piracy was a constant threat around Cornish coasts, as it had always been, but now intensified as James neglected the navy and the coastal defences, to the detriment of the seamen, fishermen and merchants who relied on the ships for their trade. The seventeenth-century Cornish, however, were becoming stronger in voicing their opinions and complaints where and when it mattered.

There was now a new influence which was to prove a great stimulus to the minds of the people – the appearance of the first edition of the Bible in English, to be given pride of place in Stuart homes. It was an incentive for all to learn to read it for themselves for the first time. Carved bible boxes to house the family Bible made their appearance, with a sloping lid on which the book was rested for the daily reading. Not only the gentry, with their private chapels, but also many less priv-ileged families now started the day with prayers and Bible readings at six in the morning. This developed into an independence of thought promoting both discussion and dissension. As a result, many different religious views were developing that were frowned upon by the Anglican Church.

These were the people, eloquent and ardent, who took an ever-increasing interest in the politics of the country. There were men of ability and courage among their number. Many Cornishmen, lawyers and merchants, now stood for Parliament, feeling a need to have their say in matters that affected them outside their own county.

Elizabeth had appreciated and encouraged the loyalty of her Cornish subjects both in the countryside and at sea. She understood them and considered all Cornishmen as her loyal courtiers. This was something that James I never understood. He refused to grant toleration either inside or outside the Church. While the Cornish knew very well that money was needed to improve the navy, they refused to pay the 'Ship-money' tax when it was introduced by Charles I, considering it illegal. The men who opposed the King did so as a matter of principle rather than for the money involved.

One of the Cornishmen who opposed first James I and then Charles I so strongly in Parliament was Sir John Eliot, Earl of St Germans. His home, Port Eliot, had come into the family's possession after the dissolution, having been first a monastery founded by St Germanus in the fifth century, when he was sent to Britain to combat the heresy of the Pelagians. Later it became an Augustinian priory. Port Eliot, to be the home of the family for the next four hundred years, was built on this ancient site. The nearby Norman church of St Germans was the cathedral seat of the bishops of Cornwall until the see was transferred to Exeter in 1043.

Sir John Eliot was one of the greatest parliamentarians of the time. Seeing the sorry state of the navy under the Stuarts, he became a champion of constitutional rights, particularly in connection with loans forced on the people. He declared, 'Upon this dispute not alone our lands and goods are engaged, but all that we call ours. These rights, these privileges, which made our fathers freemen, are in question. If they be not more carefully preserved they will render us to posterity less free, less worthy than our fathers.' These were words that stirred the hearts of many, but none more so than Cornish hearts.

The situation between King and Parliament continued to deteriorate, to the point where in 1629 Members of Parliament were forced to hold down the Speaker, while they passed the resolution that 'Whoever raises

Painting of Sir Bevil Grenville at Prideaux Place, Padstow

tax by tonnage and poundage shall be deemed a capital enemy to this Commonwealth; whoever pays such a tax shall be deemed a betrayer of liberty and an enemy of the Commonwealth'.

Sir John Eliot and his friends were imprisoned for their part in this. He died in the Tower refusing to change his views, and Charles refused permission for his son to take his father's body back to his home in Cornwall for burial, a Cornishman's greatest wish.

The Cornish Members of the Long Parliament in 1640 were led by Sir Bevil Grenville of Stowe and Sir Alexander Carew of Antony. At first all united for the common good. Sir Alexander was a strong Puritan and Sir Bevil was the best example of a 'King's' man at the beginning of the Civil War. His home at Stowe near Kilkhampton was described as half castle and half dwelling-house, situated on the cliffs looking down to Tintagel, a home halfway between the Middle Ages and the new spirit that reached to the far north coast of Cornwall. He had no desire to rebuild his home. His efforts to improve Stowe included new windows with mullions of Cornish moorstone, and he beautified it with pictures, furnishings and damasks purchased when he was away in London. He improved the grounds, planting a hop garden and an orchard. He was a greatly loved employer and landlord, and happily married to Grace, a Devonshire girl from Heavitree in Exeter, to whom he wrote, 'I have nothing in the world pleasing delightful or contenting to me but yr selfe, in you my love did begin and must end'.

When he was away from home his wife had to cope with the not always safe arrival of his purchases from London. One case of pictures was damaged before it arrived. It included one of the King and one of his friend, Sir John Eliot, which caused his wife some worry. 'I pray you make haste and come home, so God keep you well and be not angry with me.'

When Sir Bevil ordered expensive turkey work as coverings for stools and chairs, he said he would buy it 'if money hold out'. The Cornish gentry of the seventeenth century did not own vast estates and were comparatively poor by English standards. Turkey work was very popular in the seventeenth century, so obviously he wanted his Cornish home to be furnished in the latest fashion. It was a knotted wool textile, the technique of which was imitated from imported Turkish carpets.

Even when war came and Sir Bevil was away from Stowe, his thoughts were still back at his home. He sent a box of sweetmeats to his wife, the best he could get, 'except apricots'. He sent pear grafts for his orchard with instructions to his wife to tell his men to use any means necessary to keep the pigs out of the orchard. Always a hospitable man, he wrote to his wife while he was away as to the hospitality to be given to a Doctor Coxe. 'Lodge him in the Redd chamber – let some trusty body see his bed well furnished with neat linen and all things apper-tayning sweet and cleane with good fyres beneath and above.' It seems that the well-ordered and peaceful life of Stowe continued in war as it had in peace.

As opinions gradually formed into opposing factions in Parliament, at first many Members with moderate views retired to their country homes, not wishing to pledge themselves to any one party at this stage. Both Sir Richard Vyvyan of Trelowarren near the Helford River and Sir Bevil returned to their Cornish homes, but were soon to be actively involved in the inevitable Civil War. Sir Richard commanded a fort guarding the Helford River, financing the building of the fort himself. In June 1642, Sir Bevil, with Sir John Arundell of Trerice and others, was given a 'Commission of Array' by the King. The principal families of Cornwall, long-time servants of the King, became the Royalist Party, along with their followers and tenants and most of the people of Cornwall, who displayed a Celtic reverence for their king. They included all but two of the Arundells, Godolphins, Killigrews and the Bassetts of St Michael's Mount.

Thomas and Francis Arundell, Lord Robartes and Edmund Prideaux were on the Parliamentary side. As had happened in the religious disputes of the last century, the ancient families of Cornwall were no longer united as they had been in the past.

The King's forces were under the command of Sir Ralph Hopton, and under his leadership their early successes were in the main due to the strength and courage of the Cornishmen in the army, especially the Cornish pikemen. They became famous for the Celtic qualities of their fighting strength, their religious discipline and their devotion to their leaders. At first the Cornishmen showed their reluctance to cross the border into Devon and would rather defend their own county and their homes as had their Celtic ancestors before them. They even doubted whether it was lawful for them to be employed to fight outside their county. They were ultimately willing to follow their leaders wherever they were led, and it was agreed that the Cornish army would fight as part of the larger Royalist force beyond the Tamar – an historic moment in Cornish history. They were especially willing to do this when their leader was the much-loved Sir Bevil.

By the time they moved into Devon they had left Cornwall cleared of the Parliamentarians and solidly in the hands of the Royalists. They marched into Somerset, occupied Taunton and Bridgwater, but experienced great losses. They fought a battle at Lansdown Hill where Sir Bevil was killed leading a charge up the hill. The Royalists won this battle and pressed on to further victories, but with heavy Cornish losses. With the loss of Sir Bevil and several of the Cornish leaders, the heart seemed to go out of the Cornish forces. The enthusiasm for the war declined in Cornwall and their soldiers began to think of their undefended homes and coastline, and the crops waiting to be harvested. In spite of their losses they had fought bravely on, through Devon to Plymouth. The King sent them a 'Declaration unto all his loving subjects in the County of Cornwall', thanking them for their extraordinary zeal, patience and courage in his cause, and ordered copies to be published in every church, where they were to be kept, 'That as long as the History of these Times and this Nation shall continue, the Memory of how much that county hath merited from Us and Our Crown may be derived with it to Posterity'. This message still stands in some Cornish churches.

As the fortunes of both sides in the struggle rose and fell, the Roundhead armies under Oliver Cromwell turned the tide against the Royalists in 1644. The Royalist army under Essex finally capitulated at Lostwithiel in Cornwall in September. The King was unable to come to terms either with the army or Parliament, which led eventually to his trial and execution. The Royalists of Cornwall had given much to the King's cause – not only their lives, but much of their wealth as well. They were to suffer still more when the war ended because of the fines they had to pay when the King was defeated, about a tenth of the value of their estates. The amounts paid show that few of these estates were large.

Many of their homes had been plundered by the Parliamentary forces. At Menabilly near Fowey, the sixty-roomed home of the Rashleigh family, built at the beginning of the century, all the clothing was taken, along with all the jewellery and silver. Pictures of the King and Queen were slashed. The house was entirely rebuilt in the next century.

Some large houses built at this time were fortunate and still stand today. The Robartes family of Truro, traders in wood and tin rose to

The kitchen at Lanhydrock

power through the prosperity of the tin industry at the beginning of the seventeenth century, when the output of Cornish tin increased nearly two and a half times. In 1616 Richard Robartes received a knighthood and in 1620, the year the Pilgrim Fathers set sail for America, the family bought the manor of Lanhydrock, overlooking the valley of the River Fowey. In 1624 John Robartes was created Baron Robartes of Truro, a title for which he paid £10,000. This was arranged by the Duke of Buckingham. When he was later disgraced, Lord Robartes explained that the money was for a special service for the King. He began building the house at Lanhydrock in keeping with his new position. By 1642 the house had been completed by his son John, who was immediately caught up in the Civil War, which was to change the fortunes of the family for some years. At the outbreak of the war, he stationed a garrison at Lanhydrock and led his own regiment in various battles until he returned to his home in 1644. From that moment his fortunes failed. The Roundhead army he had supported was almost driven into the sea, and in August both the house and land at Lanhydrock were occupied and possessed by Sir Richard Grenville. The royal mint was established at Truro for one year during the Civil War and the silver plate in the house was melted down for the Royalists' funds. The Robartes family became prisoners at Lanhydrock, Sir John escaping by sea with other Parliamentary leaders.

A decisive battle in the war was fought at Castle Dore on 31 August 1644. The Parliamentary forces under Essex had been pushed further and further west. Loyalists in the extreme west were marching eastwards, and Essex had little option but to go south towards Fowey. His army made a stand at the hillfort, where they were utterly routed. Essex joined Lord Robartes and others escaping in a fishing boat to Plymouth.

The next year a treaty of surrender by the Royalists was signed at Truro. The last to surrender were Sir John Arundell of Trerice and the garrison of Pendennis Castle, who held out for another two months, when starvation alone forced them to surrender. Then, led by Sir John 'Jack for the King', they marched out with their horses and arms, 'colours flying, trumpets sounding, drums beating, matches lighted at both ends, and bullets in their mouths' – the end of the Civil War in Cornwall.

When Lord Robartes returned to Lanhydrock he occupied himself in improving his estate and finishing the work he had started before war began. He planted an avenue of sycamores in 1648 and completed the gatehouse at the entrance to the park which bears his initials and those of his wife Lucy. The Robartes family were to occupy the house until 1969. It is now open to the public and owned by the National Trust.

Not all Puritans stayed at home in the seventeenth century. Cornish Puritans and Quakers made some of their first journeys to America at this time, taking with them all that was best in the way of life they left behind. Their wives were well fitted to cope with the pioneering life ahead. They were the end product of centuries of self-sufficiency in Cornish homes. Together with their strong religious background, the domestic ideals they took with them now became the foundation of the American home. The hall or living room in their New England homes they called 'the keeping room', a term going back to the medieval castle keep – the safe retreat for the family in times of trouble.

Lawrence Growden, a Quaker pewterer from St Merryn, near Padstow, sailed from Fowey in his own ship, with his brother Joseph, family and servants, forty-five in all. They arrived in Pennsylvania in

1684 after a crossing lasting nineteen weeks. He gave the name of the home he left at Trevose to his new home, a large estate on the Neshaming Creek. He returned to Cornwall in 1708 to die, as was the wish of many Cornishmen when forced to spend time out of the county. Many Cornish names that have died out in the county can be found among families in America.

Those who remained in England suffered the penalties of not complying with the law. Their goods were continually distrained as they refused to pay tithes, held meetings in their homes and refused to attend church. Many had their working tools taken from them in lieu of payment. They were liable to lose their firearms, farm implements, clothing, bedding and furniture. The followers of George Fox, the founder of the Society of Friends, the Quakers, suffered continual persecution for their beliefs in the second half of the century.

The focus of Quakerism in Cornwall was the home of a farmer's wife at Tregangeeves, a farmhouse two miles to the west of St Austell. Here Loveday Hambly lived and farmed. She was the daughter of an old and distinguished Cornish family. From 1656, when she first visited George Fox while he was imprisoned in Launceston prison, until her death, her home was the meeting place for Quakers on their way to visit Fox in prison, and later a resting place for many Quakers on their visits to Cornwall. The grey farmhouse became famous for the hospitality of its mistress, now a widow – 'her tables were always largely and plentifully spread'. This cannot have been easy to achieve as her household utensils of pewter, brass and copper were continually taken from her when she refused to pay the fines levied on her. She was imprisoned on several occasions, sometimes for months at a time, and repeatedly suffered the loss of cows, horses and calves from her farm. The punishments were the same for rich and poor. For attending a Quaker meeting, Joane Robyns was about to have her last crock, in which she was boiling her meat, taken from her, 'there beinge hardly any goods else in ye house worth distraineigne', but she was eventually allowed to keep her pot after promising to pay the five-shilling fine. In spite of all Loveday suffered she lived to be seventy-eight, dying in 1682. The entry recording her death states 'Loveday Hambly, long time famous for her hospitality and good works'.

Travelling in Cornwall at this time cannot have been easy for men of any religion, but travel they did. Riding was more a necessity than a recreation. The first reference to a coach in Cornwall is to the one in which Charles I came to the county in 1644. The Hawkins family from Trewinnard near St Erth were the owners of one of the first coaches in west Cornwall, built in about 1700. It can now be seen in Truro Museum. Such was the state of the roads that six or more men had to accompany it, armed with poles, ropes, picks and spades to extract the coach when it became stuck in holes.

One intrepid traveller on horseback journeyed to Cornwall during her travels round England at the end of the century. This was Celia Fiennes, a Puritan lady, who said she travelled both for the good of her health and the improvement of her conversation. One of Cornwall's first tourists in 1697, she rode from Looe to Fowey, her horse struggling through the quagmires formed in the bad September weather. The houses at St Austell she described as like barns 'up to the top of the house' (the continuance of the medieval hall house), but there was a pretty dining room and chamber and 'very neate Country women'.

She was much cheered by her landlady there producing the first West Country tart she had been able to obtain, although she had asked for one in Devonshire and Somerset. 'An apple pye with a custard all on the top, its ye most acceptable entertainment it cd be made me. They scald their creame and milk in most part of these countries and so its a sort of clouted creame as we call it, with a little sugar and soe put on ye top of ye apple pye.'

Although well pleased with her supper, she was not so pleased with 'the custom of the country wch is a universall smoaking, both men, women and children have all the pipes of tobacco in their mouths and soe sit round the fire smoaking...'

As early as 1603 tobacco smoking had been condemned unsuccessfully by James I as 'A custom loathsome to the eye, hateful to the nose, harmful to the brain, dangerous to the lungs and in the black stinking fumes thereof nearest resembling the black stygian smoke of the pit that is bottomless'. This royal message appears not to have reached Cornwall by the end of the century, when the habit was well established in the whole family.

Tobacco was only one of the many imports that came into the ports of Cornwall in increasing amounts in the seventeenth century, showing the growing economy of the county and the desire of the people to have more and more possessions in their homes and more of the materials to improve them. Bricks and window glass, fire grates, lanterns, candlesticks, kitchen utensils, pots and pans, earthenware, glasses, glass bottles, household bedding and clothes arrived at Cornish ports in large amounts from all over the world. The importing of paper increased as well as books, maps, stationery and pictures. Many of these items furnished the homes of both farmers and the merchants who now lived in the larger ports, which grew in size as the century continued. Loveday Hambly had seventeen printed maps taken from her home in payment of a fine for holding a meeting in there.

While many who had fought in the war were rewarded with knighthoods, many more were impoverished by the help they had given and on returning to their homes had to face many years of litigation to repossess their properties after sequestration by the Parliamentary forces. Others prospered at first but ever-changing conditions meant that no one's position was secure for long.

Bad harvests after the war did not help the people and plague returned to Cornwall in 1646. At St Ives parcels of food, marked with the prices to be paid, were brought from surrounding districts and laid beside the streams that bounded the infected area. The people of St Ives paid for the food by putting their money in the streams when they collected it. Five hundred and thirty-five inhabitants of St Ives died at this time, a third of the population of the town.

When Charles I was executed on 30 January 1649, a great storm arose in Cornwall. The Steeple Rock at Land's End was thrown down. The ship carrying the King's wardrobe and furniture belonging to the royal family, on its way to France, was wrecked on Godrevy Island in St Ives Bay. The sixty people aboard were all drowned. It was as if Cornwall itself was protesting at the tragic death of their king.

During the Restoration, Sir Bevil's son, Sir John Grenville, became Earl of Bath. He pulled down the original house at Stowe and in its place he built a great classical house in brick, said to be one of the largest and finest houses in Cornwall. It was beautifully furnished, but unlike the old house, it brought no good fortune to its subsequent owners and was hardly ever inhabited. Sir John died in 1701 with his fortunes waning. This was a state of affairs his son and heir was unable to bear. He shot himself a fortnight after his father's death and both were buried on the same day at Kilkhampton. The grandson became the third and last Earl of Bath and within ten years he was also dead. The first earl's daughter had the house pulled down and everything sold. Some of the fine panelling and carvings were later installed in Prideaux Place, Padstow by Edmund Prideaux. Now little remains of one of the most beautiful houses to have stood on the north Cornish coast.

Sidney Godolphin, of Godolphin Hall between Marazion and Helston, was happily married to Margaret, a friend of John Evelyn, the diarist. Sadly she died in childbirth in London in 1678 at the age of twenty-five, after only three years of marriage. Her husband was overcome with grief at her death from puerperal fever, a common risk in seventeenth-century childbirth. So stricken was he that he was unable to travel all the way with her coffin on its long journey from London to Cornwall, for she had expressed a wish to be buried at Godolphin. John Evelyn left an account of the sad journey of the hearse to Breage Church, drawn by six horses and accompanied by about thirty of her relations and servants, including her husband's brother, Sir William, two more of his brothers and three sisters. The coffin was taken out of the hearse every night and placed in a house, attended by her servants and candles. The funeral cost not much less than £1,000. At the end of the century Sidney was married again, this time to the eldest daughter of the Duke of Marlborough. Godolphin, as Queen Anne's Lord Treasurer and First Minister, financed Marlborough's campaigns, and as long as Marlborough was in the Queen's favour Godolphin House in Cornwall was safe. But in 1710 Anne quarrelled with the Marlboroughs and Godolphin lost his office. He died two years later and the house gradually fell into decay until rescued by subsequent owners. The greatest days of yet another Cornish home were over.

Lanhydrock was more fortunate. The north wing of the house that Lord Robartes completed in 1642 still stands, together with the two-storey entrance porch, but the rest was destroyed by fire in 1881. Luckily the greatest room of the original house remains untouched by the fire. This is the gallery, a room popular with the Elizabethans, where families could take their exercise and recreation when the weather was inclement. It runs the extent of the north wing on the first floor, a length of thirty-five metres, well lit by its tall windows, originally with panelled walls and with the most spectacular plaster ceiling, which is still intact. It has twenty-four panels depicting incidents in the Old Testament from the creation of the world to the burial of Isaac. The plasterwork is probably the work of a family of plasterers, the Abbot family from Bideford, whose work is found in many houses in Devon and Cornwall. The house, as it was rebuilt after the fire, gives a complete picture of a late Victorian home, with its domestic quarters.

Not only did they enjoy walking indoors in the seventeenth century, but ornamental walks outdoors became a feature of gardens. Promenading one such walk while staying at Bodinnick during the Civil War nearly ended the life of Charles I on his visit to Cornwall in August 1644. The walk by the River Fowey, still known as the 'Hall Walk', was within range of musket shot from Fowey and, shortly after the King had passed by, a fisherman was killed at the same spot.

The ordinary people of Cornwall settled down to their normal way of life in the homes they had never been very eager to leave in order to fight outside their county. They were staunch supporters of their Cornish leaders and had fought bravely with them, but when many of these great men were killed the desire of their followers to return to their Cornish homes was paramount in their minds.

The downfall of the monarchy had the effect of leaving Cornwall not only without a king, but also without a duke. The duchy was abolished after the death of the King and many of its manors were sold, to be restored only when the monarchy was restored in 1660. The purchasers of duchy lands were evicted, although some were given new leases under the duchy.

The restoration of the monarchy was greatly welcomed by the Cornish. The county had changed during the war and the rule of the government that followed. The Catholics had declined in power – the Quakers and Puritans were stronger – but the Church of England was well established in the minds of the people. The Cornish people, however, had survived all that had happened, with the momentous events of the seventeenth century making little difference to their fundamental beliefs in themselves.

When James II issued the Declaration of Indulgence in 1688, granting toleration to Catholics, religious differences were once more roused in Cornwall. Bishop Trelawny of Trelawne protested and was prepared to stand trial rather than deny his principles. All Cornishmen were prepared to fight for his right to do this, regardless of what his principles were. They were never called upon to do so as the bishop was acquitted. The incident inspired Parson Hawker, Vicar of Morwenstow, to write his famous lines:

> And have they fixed the where and when?
> And shall Trelawny die?
> Here's twenty thousand Cornish men
> Will know the reason why!
> (from the poem *Song of the Western Men*)

CHAPTER 9

Mines, Minerals and Miners

AFTER THE TRAUMATIC events of the seventeenth century, the Celtic Cornish settled down to concentrate on what they did best, making the most of the rocks and minerals, land and sea, that were the real foundation of their county. These had supported them from prehistoric times. The mines reached the height of their production in the eighteenth century. This brought about great changes in homes, work and the environment during the next hundred years.

For centuries the mines had been worked mainly by individual miners or small groups, many living in isolation in their moorland cottages. Many of these cottages were built in the days when 'Do it yourself' extended in Cornwall to building a simple home overnight with the help of friends, whereby a young couple could then claim the freehold of it. They added to the building bit by bit if and when their circumstances improved. Most of these were one-room cottages with cob walls of mud and straw and a thatched roof. Unless stone was available, these homes needed to be rebuilt time and again on the same spot, as the original building decayed.

Writing in the sixteenth century, Richard Carew described these cottages as hovels with 'walls of earth, low thatched roofs, few partitions, no planchings or glass windows, and scarcely any chimneys other than a hole in the wall to let out the smoke, their bed, straw and a blanket'.

Where stone was used, the walls had a chance of longer life. They could be lined with wattle and daub for extra warmth, as their ancestors had done centuries before. Where slate was available, as in the Delabole district, this was preferred to thatch, because of the danger of fire. Nothing that the county could produce was wasted.

At the homes in Delabole near the quarry, good use was made of the slate produced, as it had been at Harlyn in the Celtic Iron Age. It was used for hearths, porches, doorways and mantelpieces, as well as for floors, window sills, cisterns and storage chests, kitchen utensils, rolling

Delabole Slate Quarry in 1875

pins and chopping boards. Many of the slate floors are still in position today. Cornish slate was exported by sea to other parts of England as well as to Europe. The slatebed of Delabole is 345 million years old. It has a depth of over 150 metres and is a mile in circumference. It has been continuously worked since the Middle Ages.

Most miners' cottages had a small garden attached, often a pigsty at the side and a rick of furze or turf for burning in the hearth. Even in the smallest cottage, the hearth was the heart of the home. Where a chimney was practical, it was built as large as possible, often out of all proportion to the size of the room, sometimes with a built-in seat at the side, often just a tree trunk. Cooking was done on a simple brandise placed in the hot ashes, with bread baked on an iron slab under a bake-iron, or in a cloam oven.

As mining communities grew, probably most relied on local markets for much of their food and other needs.

The cottages were built sometimes to work in, and always for shelter, in which to rest at the end of a hard day. One thing is certain – Cornish cottages built simply for the enjoyment of the countryside or the view of the sea and shore were unknown. In every cottage in the eighteenth century was a worker and his family fighting for existence.

Wives and children worked to supplement the tin miner's wages. The women worked as 'bal maids', breaking up medium-sized pieces of rock with hammers. The children helped to wash it. The boys went underground as early as twelve years of age to learn to be miners.

In 1850 the average age of those buried in the mining village of St Just-in-Penwith was twenty-seven, for both men and women.

A surgeon visited a miner's home in 1778 to which the injured man had been carried after one of the all-too-common accidents in a mine. He found the hut full of naked children 'destitute of all conveniences and almost of all necessaries'. Fatalities were constant from falling rock and falls from ladders. In the Gwennap copper mines, one in five miners met a violent death. This was the price paid for the fact that Gwennap mine yielded more copper and tin than any other in the world.

Tragedies were frequent with small children left at home alone. Sleeping accommodation for them was often only boards placed under the roof and across beams – the 'talfat'. This sometimes had a plank nailed across for protection, or simply a railing to prevent children falling to the room below.

In spite of the hardships and poverty, many Cornish housewives managed to retain a reputation for cleanliness.

By the beginning of the century, the demand for tin had so increased that the mines became owned by large landowners. They had the money needed to develop them and purchase the machinery now available to do this. They acquired great wealth from the mines on their land, attracting others. Mining companies were formed, financially organized with bankers, farmers and merchants joining them. This development not only changed the face of Cornwall, but also the way in which many of the people lived and where they lived.

Even in the fifteenth century underground mining was becoming more important than the streaming methods of earlier times. Shafts were being sunk and already some mines were employing hundreds of men. All machinery, such as hoisting gear, pumps to deal with water problems, mills to supply supporting posts, was labour intensive. The

East Pool Mine in 1893 at the 180 fathoms level

only power available was water-wheels, men or horses.

Celia Fiennes took a great interest in the methods of the tin miners on her journey to St Austell in 1698. She described how they took the ore and pounded it in a stamping mill, then flung it into a furnace with coal to make the fire. Before the first imports of coal, the forests of

Cornwall were almost cleared of wood to supply the furnaces. The metal was separated from the coal by the great heat and fell into a trench below, then to be poured into moulds. She wrote how the hard work down the shafts had to be continuous night and day to prevent the mines from flooding.

She noted that copper was mined in the same way as tin, but was sent to Wales and Bristol to be smelted owing to the shortage of fuel in Cornwall.

In 1710 the government lifted the duty on sea-borne coal to Cornwall, and its use in homes and mines was facilitated. The use of coal for smelting involved importing it, so as in the mining industry this activity also came into the hands of the merchants who supplied it.

In 1727 Sir John St Aubyn of St Michael's Mount improved the harbour there to promote the export of Cornish tin. Norwegian ships sailed into the harbour with timber, as a great deal was needed for shoring up mine workings.

Many mines were open-cast trenches and were worked as such until recent times, but as mines were sunk ever deeper, water was an increasing problem. Solving this occupied Cornish inventors throughout the seventeenth century. They provided a variety of pumps to improve the situation. These pumps often drained wells dry and made it necessary for water to be brought from as much as three miles away. The water situation was no better in towns, especially in summer, causing a long wait at wells and leading to heated arguments.

Adits were constructed to drain water away from the mine workings with leather buckets hoisting water from the lower levels to the adit. When gunpowder was available at the end of the century, it was used to blast longer adits much faster than was previously possible. However, gunpowder added to the many dangers to which miners could be subject. Only when a safety fuse was invented were many disasters avoided.

There was now an increase in the population of towns and ports in Cornwall for the first time. As their businesses grew, the gentry and merchants acquired property in the towns and ports and workers were soon attracted there by the growing industry. The ports had always been busy with the fishing industry, but now they were bustling with the increase in trade and in ships to carry the ore.

Cottage-owners may often have lived in great poverty in the countryside, but their plight was probably no worse than that of the workers who now lived in the back streets of Truro, Penzance and Bodmin.

At least the country cottages had fresh air in abundance, hopefully fresh food from their small gardens, and fuel for heating and cooking. The town-dwellers were more likely to have offal and manure stacked in their back yards and drains that were open sewers spreading typhus, cholera and smallpox.

Many of the roofs of town houses were also of slate instead of thatch, to prevent damage by fire. They were often decorated with ridge tiles with a knight on horseback, or little pixies who were said to dance on the roof at midnight, a sound more probably due to rats in the rafters, of which Carew had complained centuries before. Large roof slates in Cornwall often had one end left ragged, as can be seen on the roof at Tintagel Old Post Office.

Life was so hard in the mining districts and the work so badly paid that many miners' daughters left home of necessity, to become maids in the homes of the wealthy in the towns. In fact, many women from country homes were increasingly drawn to the life, with its leisure pursuits, now offered in the larger towns. As they became richer, they wished to become part of 'The Age of Elegance', now being enjoyed in other parts of Britain. It was said that in Truro 'all modes of polished life were visible in genteel houses, elegant hospitality, fashionable apparel and cautious manners, which was unmatched elsewhere in Cornwall'. Theatres, shops, assemblies and pleasure gardens provided pastimes that, for the first time, made country life seem dull in comparison. The town houses of Truro had long strips of garden at their backs, giving their owners more space than those in poorer dwellings, which were tightly packed along narrow winding streets.

Nearby nobility and gentry visited the theatre and balls at the assembly rooms, arriving in rose-cushioned and curtained sedan chairs, stately landaus and barouches and fours.

Roads did improve somewhat in the eighteenth century, but most were little more than bridle paths. If they were to take full advantage of the attractions, during the winter months especially, many found it more convenient to move to a house in town. Lord Robartes owned a house in Boscawen Street in Truro. Here his family found a variety of interests, including the literary society and the county library, as well as the cockpit. Penzance had fortnightly assemblies for music and dancing, a theatre and a cockpit; indeed, cockfighting continued into the present century and bull-baiting almost as long.

The assembly hall in Bodmin was described in 1797 as about 7.5 metres long with uneven boards which occasionally tripped up the dancers. It was lit by candles and the music was sometimes provided by a military band, or more usually by a lone fiddler, the latter preferred by some as being less noisy than the band. As well as the social life of the gentry, there had always been great socializing between all classes in Cornwall – the professional classes were happy to discuss all the topics of the day with the tradesmen, farmers and smugglers in the local inns. This had been so since the earliest days of feasting and drinking in Celtic Cornwall.

One of the families that made a great fortune from mining was the Lemon family, who as well as their country estate at Carclew on Restronguet Creek had a town house in Princes Street in Truro, where wealthy families of the time had their fashionable homes. These houses are now shops and offices.

But the Lemon family did not spend their wealth only on their own homes, but were also great benefactors to the town of Truro. They laid out a large area of the town with thoroughfares that have been a community asset ever since: Charles Street, Mount Charles, Lemon Street, Lemon Villa and Carclew Street.

The great love of the Cornish for their homes made them anxious to improve them and make them as beautiful as money would allow. Carclew was surrounded by a garden and walks that one traveller described as 'beautiful beyond description and by far exceeding anything I have seen in Cornwall'.

Cornish hospitality extended to travellers, as it had always done, when Mr Lemon was in Truro. Some visitors to his home at Carclew in his absence, caught unexpectedly in a storm, were given supper by a servant, by a good fire without question, and then given a bed for the night – a Chinese bed in a room hung with handsome Indian wallpaper.

William Lemon bought the house in 1749 when it was half built, the previous owner having died. It was designed by Thomas Edwards, who also designed his elegant house in Princes Street. Carclew was built along classical lines, which had developed from the architectural style of the continent of Europe. Unfortunately the house was destroyed by fire in 1934, but the gardens are still enjoyed by visitors today. After the middle of the century landscape gardening was increasingly popular, and the lakes and trees laid out and planted in the eighteenth century are the foundation of the gardens seen there today.

The gardens at Prideaux Place in Padstow were laid out at the same time as those at Carclew. The earliest existing drawings are those of the formal gardens created by Edmund Prideaux in 1730. He provided added interest with a classical temple, an obelisk, a grotto and a small stone arbour with Roman funerary urns dated AD 50, which he brought back from Italy on his grand tour, a tour made by many wealthy young men at this time. The ideas they saw in Europe were introduced both into their gardens and into the decoration of their homes.

In the manner of every new generation, his son Humphry removed the obelisk and landscaped the gardens in the style of Capability Brown, who replanned many famous gardens with sweeps of open country and strategically placed trees, lakes and small buildings. A pastel portrait of Humphry hangs in the family's sitting room, painted by the celebrated Italian artist Rosalba Carrier when when he was on his grand tour in the mid-eighteenth century. She fell in love with him, but he never knew of her love. Only when the picture was cleaned in 1914 was a letter to him telling him of her love found concealed behind the frame.

The gardens are again extensively restored by the present owner, Peter Prideaux-Brune, works that include rescuing from the under-growth an ornate Italian flower garden and an ornamental pond which was under decades of sludge and slime. The family are also restoring the Elizabethan house that is their family home and which has been occu-pied by the Prideaux family since Nicholas Prideaux secured the estate in 1535. The name of Brune was added at the end of the century when there was a marriage to one of the many heiresses who increased the family fortunes – a usual way of increasing wealth from the Middle Ages onwards. These ladies of the Prideaux family are represented in heraldic form in the stained-glass windows of the library. The original house had eighty-one rooms, forty-four of which were bedrooms. The house was occupied by the American Army in the Second World War, and only six of these have been redecorated so far.

The original house was finished in 1592, but the classical ideas that were influencing Edmund Prideaux and many other Cornish owners caused him to remove the pointed gables on the entrance front and put in sash windows and grates suitable for coal fires. The misfortunes that had befallen the house of Stowe now benefited Prideaux Place which purchased and installed its panelling and staircase. At the beginning of the next century, Edmund's grandson again made changes and created the drawing room, hall and library. Although many miles from London, Prideaux Place kept up with all the developments in the rest of the country. The family produced many distinguished lawyers through the years who no doubt were always closely in touch with London tastes. As in the Middle Ages, disputes over ownership of property and wealth were still rife as the value of Cornish estates increased.

The present renovations at the house will include work on painted panels in the drawing room featuring Cornish scenes. There are three inset paintings there by Antonio Verrio removed from the dining room at Stowe, together with carving by Grinling Gibbons, as well as the Earl of Bath's wine cooler. These are now in the Grenville Room at Prideaux Place, where hangs a portrait of the well-loved Sir Bevil Grenville, the cousin of Edmund, with whom there was a close relationship in spite of the fact that they had been on opposite sides in the Civil War.

The great chamber of the house still has its original sixteenth century ceiling, discovered when an eighteenth-century successor that had been hung below it was removed. It depicts the biblical story of Susannah and the elders and was executed by the Allott family, who had worked on the ceiling in the gallery at Lanhydrock.

Hospitality in the great houses of the time was generous, but was also so in smaller homes and farmhouses. A visit by William Beckford to the home of a Cornish squire in 1787 provided him with a meal of 'a savoury pig and some of the finest poultry I ever tasted and round the table two or three brace of old Cornish gentle folks, not deficient in humour or originality'. The food had been prepared in a number of halls, pantries and ante-chambers through which the guests had been escorted while on a rambling tour of the house. Usually by this time in the larger houses, the kitchens were as far away from the elegant living rooms as possible. Gone were the days of feasting and cooking in the same communal hall. Lukewarm food must have been the order of the day, although closed trolleys were sometimes used to wheel the food to the dining room. After dinner the party was entertained by a cockfight, which William Beckford was pleased to see didn't stain the room or the guests with blood, as the cocks were unarmed and had had their spurs cut short.

While the hall of the newer houses was now little more than an entrance containing the staircase, which was now in the centre of the house leading to the upper bedrooms, there were homes where the living room was still called the hall. New buildings had elegant sash windows, which in Cornwall were usually of the lateral sliding type.

One of the best examples of an eighteenth-century house in Cornwall is Antony House, built in 1721, and the home of the Carew family since the fifteenth century. The house that Richard Carew lived in and wrote about in the sixteenth century no longer exists, with the exception of some panelling in the hall, where the portrait of Richard Carew looks down on visitors today. The present house was built by Sir William Carew after the family had survived their troubles in the Civil War, when two members were beheaded. It stands in 250 acres of land on the River Lynher, a tributary of the Tamar, the river enjoyed by Richard Carew, along with the fish ponds he constructed. The gardens were laid out in the late eighteenth century by the fashionable landscape gardener Humphry Repton, giving a wonderful view from the terrace of the house. The estate later passed to the Pole-Carew family and was handed over to the National Trust in 1961 to be enjoyed by the public. The brick house is covered with grey Pentewan stone from Mevagissey and is full of eighteenth-century tapestries, china, furniture and embroideries.

Such luxuries were not for everyone. In Penzance it is said there was only one house with a carpet and floors were for the most part sprinkled with sand. This was also used for scouring pans, especially the copper pans and moulds so much in use for desserts and sweets.

Verdigris in these was a great danger and people died from it. Although forks were in use now, there was not a single silver fork in Penzance. During the Civil War the royal mint was established in Truro and much of Cornwall's domestic silver was melted down in the war effort.

In 1752 Dr Borlase, an eminent historian, went with a Dr Lyttelton on horseback to supper with Lady Vyvyan at Trelowarren, the house that had been in her family since 1426. The house had been restored and enlarged after the Civil War. The two gentlemen described the large entrance hall 'furnished with calvers, hunting poles, militia drums and stag horns'. The works of several generations of the ladies of the family were evident in cloth hangings. and lace bed covers. But the greatest curiosity seen on their visit was the old lady herself, surrounded by her children and grandchildren. The Cornish custom of kissing everyone, young and old, was performed by the visitors, after which they were rewarded with a cup of sack. They then attended prayers in the chapel, which took place twice a day. At supper in the parlour later, the old lady ate a pound of Scotch collops and was surprised her visitors did not manage to do the same. The meat and poultry were likely to have been tough, having walked every mile of the way to market; often they were bad as well, because of poor storage conditions. Meat was served highly spiced to disguise this, but the spices were expensive and kept under lock and key in special spice boxes and cupboards. In towns the milk was brought round by milkmaids with yokes over their shoulders. The buckets of milk that hung from either end were often uncovered. More vegetables were eaten than in the past, and the introduction of the turnip, as a food for people and animals, enabled cattle to be kept through the winter to provide fresh meat, instead of all meat having to be salted down in the autumn.

Two innovations of this time have remained with us – the coffee break in the morning and a light lunch eaten at midday, the evening meal being taken later and later as the century progressed. The popularity of coffee-drinking grew apace with an increasing number of coffee shops opening in the larger towns. By the middle of the century, tea, bread and cheese had become the staple diet of the poor. In the larger homes, the tea-making ceremony was usually carried out in the sitting room, the brew made by the lady of the house herself from tea kept in her own locked caddy. The leaves were often used again by the servants and then sold to the poor at the back door.

This tea-drinking resulted in many more acquisitions for the home. There had to be small tables, tea-pots, tea cups, saucers, plates and spoons for this new pastime. By the end of the century, Josiah Wedgwood was producing pottery in such quantities that it was brought within the reach of many. Pewterware was now relegated to the kitchen for the use of the servants. Wedgwood had used Lizard soapstone in his search for a finer and whiter soft-paste porcelain, but it was William Cookworthy, the Quaker chemist from Plymouth, who by 1768 used the china clay and china stone of Cornwall to perfect the first British hard-paste porcelain with clay from Breage and St Austell.

Wedgwood also enhanced the appearance of the ladies drinking their tea by supplying the paste for making china teeth, where formerly the toothless wealthy had false teeth on plates made of wood, bone or ivory. Teeth were a constant problem, and fans for ladies to hide their rotten teeth, to say nothing of their bad breath, were very popular.

The terms formerly used for brewing beer, the mainstay of feasting in earlier Celtic days, now attached themselves to the ritual of tea-making. The tea was said to be 'brewed' or 'mashed', the latter term originally used for pouring boiling water on to the malt in brewing ale.

It seems that every increase in the standard of living was accompanied by an increase in the number of articles needed to do the work, all of them needing cleaning. This was not a problem the mistress of the house had to worry about; there was always plenty of labour available to do it. Some of the kitchen work gradually became easier. Spits could now be turned by a clockwork spit jack wound up by a key. The joint was suspended underneath and revolved vertically instead of horizontally. Vertical cooking became necessary when the fire was confined in a narrower space behind bars as coal became more usual.

Slaving over a hot stove was not for the wealthier ladies of fashion who attended the assemblies in the towns. The exaggerated hairstyles at the beginning of the century caused many problems. It was not unknown for them to catch fire if the owner sat too near a candle flame, so wearing them for cooking must have been out of the question.

If life among the gentry was becoming ever more genteel, the life of the poor became even coarser as the century continued. They were forced to work harder and longer for the small wages they took home. Spending hours climbing down the mines to their work and hours again climbing up at the end of the day when cold and tired, often walking miles back to their homes, reduced them to old men if they were lucky enough to live to forty.

Smuggling and wrecking were increasingly resorted to at this time, with everyone being involved. There was no need for ships to be lured on to the rocks to be wrecked by lights shining from the cliffs, as is often believed. It is possible this happened when men were desperate, but the coastline of Cornwall and the wild seas provided many opportunities for ships to flounder on the treacherous rocks, without additional help from the watchers on the shore. There were always watchers on the lookout for a ship in distress. Wrecks were a valuable addition to the income of the lords of coastal manors, but their valuable cargoes often went to whoever reached them first.

The smuggling of luxury goods obtained in exchange for tin bene-fited many. The gentry and clergy were ever grateful for duty-free brandy or tea and happy to encourage the activity. The rocks around the coast provided many hiding places for such goods.

The arrival in Cornwall in 1743 of the Methodist John Wesley and his brother Charles did much to change the habits of the people. Wesley found Cornwall a society occupied with money, fashion and easy living at the top, with suffering, great poverty and unlawfulness at the lower levels, where people relieved their troubles with violence and drink. Wesley threw himself wholeheartedly into spreading the message of Christianity, travelling miles on horseback over the rough roads. He would preach from four or five in the morning, stopping at six or more villages and towns during the day.

The Cornish people had not been happy with their churches since the Reformation. The services did not satisfy their Celtic exuberance and spiritual needs. They welcomed the Methodist approach and the fire in the speeches of the two brothers with open hearts and minds. Wesley's message brought hope. He declared, 'The more I converse with the believers in Cornwall, the more I am convinced that they had sustained great loss for want of hearing the doctrine of Christian

John Wesley

Perfection clearly and strongly enforced.'

The Wesleys suffered many attacks on their early visits to Cornwall, when they were thought to be enemies of the Church. They were not enemies, merely trying to revive the spirit of the Church, which had died. If they did not revive the churches, they succeeded in reviving the spirits of the Cornish people, filling them with great enthusiasm. Wesley was soon preaching to thousands at his meetings, not only to the poor but, as he put it, to many of 'the better sort', 'inasmuch as curled, tied and powdered hair, high heads which were before idolized, are now detested and abandoned, and the lofty looks are brought down'.

The revivalist meetings were now so large that no building could hold them. They were held outdoors, often at Gwennap pit, where Wesley preached on fifteen occasions. This pit was probably the result of the collapse of the underground mining excavations, and had wonderful acoustics, enabling Wesley's voice to reach the thousands there. Later, in 1806, circular terraces of seats were fashioned in the grassy banks.

While the Wesleys had not wished to separate themselves from the parish churches, but simply to preach in them, this became more diffi-

Gwennap Pit in 1900

cult owing to the growing antagonism of the clergy, who found themselves losing their congregations. It was inevitable that the Methodists
would have to hold their meeting in buildings of their own with enthu-
siastic preachers risen from their own communities, many drawn from
the poorest of them. By the end of the century little Methodist chapels
were found throughout the countryside. As they had built their own
cottages in earlier days, the Cornish now built their own chapels and
found many gifted preachers to fill them.

The new thoughts, education and responsibilities John Wesley had
inspired in them brought a complete change of outlook in the Cornish
as the nineteenth century dawned.

CHAPTER 10

Railways and Travellers

ORNWALL, it seems, has never failed to produce the leaders it wanted when they were needed. It was as if the early belief that King Arthur would return to help them in critical times was strong enough for them to know that 'a man for the moment' would appear at the right time. Men of great distinction did this throughout the years. Whether in religion, war or social problems, they produced the right solutions for the county, and often for the world. Such a man was Richard Trevithick.

He was born in 1771 in the heart of the mining country at Illogan, between Camborne and Redruth, the son of a Cornish mine captain. He acquired much knowledge both of the mines and pumping engines from his father, and was already employed as a consulting engineer when only nineteen.

He became friends with Davies Gilbert, a Cornishman of great scientific and mathematical ability, later to become President of the Royal Society after another Cornishman, Humphry Davy, left that office. Gilbert became Trevithick's adviser over many years.

Early pumping engines invented by Thomas Newcomen and James Watt were greatly improved by Trevithick. His wife, Jane Harvey, was from the Hayle family that built the most efficient beam engines. Trevithick was to devise many improvements and additions to this engine and to many others, including the first full-sized locomotive in Britain, built by him at Camborne in 1801, and the first locomotive to run on rails in 1804. This was the forerunner of the engines built later by George Stephenson in 1814. Richard continued to work on improving steam engines, including what became known as the 'Cornish Boiler'. This led to the 'Cornish Engine' that was to become well known all over the world.

By 1816, the Cornish love of travel and exploration found him travelling in Peru, inspecting mines and imparting his knowledge far and wide in South America.

The engine house at Levant mine

By 1828 he was in Holland, where he had been invited to help with the problem of draining the land, using the Cornish engine.

If Cornish mines were to reach the peak of production in the nineteenth century, he was the man to give them the means to achieve this.

Trevithick continued inventing right up to the time he died in Kent in 1833, while still working, leaving descendants who worked on the development of engines and boilers all over the world. He received little monetary reward for his efforts; nor did the miners who worked down the mines.

One of the greatest changes in Cornwall in the nineteenth century, for better or worse, was effected by the coming of the railways. The first continuous rail link between Penzance and London commenced on 4 May 1859. Brunel's Royal Albert Bridge across the Tamar had been officially opened by Prince Albert on 2 May.

The effect of this was not only to bring Cornwall nearer to London, but also to bring Cornish clocks in line with London time, now to be kept at all stations. Penzance had formerly been twenty-two and a half minutes and Truro twenty minutes behind London time.

Short railway lines had been in use to service the tin and copper mines for many years. These were gradually extended to take china clay to the potteries of the Midlands, and granite to all areas. The latter was used in the building of the London Embankment.

By 1866 it was possible to make the first uninterrupted journey from Penzance to Paddington, opening up the farthest tip of the country to the rest of England. The journey took eleven hours forty minutes. By 1870 it took ten hours nineteen minutes and by 1879 eight hours fifty-five minutes. In 1904 the Cornish Riviera Express made the journey in six hours thirty-five minutes. A seat could be reserved for one shilling and a five-course lunch on the train was served for two shillings and six-pence.

By the end of the century steam-heated corridor trains lit by gas were running.

By 1887 visitors were able to travel to St Ives from St Erth on the main line. The Great Western Railway acquired Tregenna Castle in St Ives to establish a hotel in the town, and the rush was on.

London was now attracting many of the fashionable people of the Cornish towns, who before the coming of the railway had been content with local assemblies and theatres.

St Ives had been at the height of its prosperity early in the century before the coming of the railway. It had flourishing mines, fishing and agriculture. The railway improved things further as traders could now send fish and early vegetables to London. In the opposite direction the first visitors did not take long to discover Cornwall.

Among them were artists, many of whom had studied in Paris, but who were now anxious to leave the ever-encroaching areas of industrialization in England and Europe, and to follow the trends to a revival of rural life. This trend led to a desire to paint country scenes not in studios but 'en plein air'. They found these scenes among the working population of rural Cornwall, and could record a way of life that they felt was fast disappearing.

In the wonderful Cornish light they could not have found a landscape asking more to be painted. They settled both in St Ives and in the fishing village of Newlyn about a mile away. St Ives was the more cosmopolitan village, but Newlyn was a quieter traditional Cornish community, which enabled the artists to set up their easels in the fresh air and paint their subjects at work in their natural surroundings.

Their leader was Stanhope Forbes, who, after working as an artist in London and France, discovered Newlyn while on a tour of Cornwall in 1886, while looking for somewhere to settle and paint. He found it 'a village which seemed the very object of my search' where 'the people seemed to fall naturally into their places and to harmonise with the surroundings'.

He was followed by many artists and friends who settled around Newlyn. Forbes himself found rooms and a studio for fifteen shillings a week, which included attendance, cooking and lights, but not coal or food. Many of the landladies provided good food and there was much Celtic feasting for the artists. At one dinner party, Forbes's landlady provided lamb with mint sauce, capon *sauce Madderne*, macaroni cheese, *tartes aux frais*, fruit and dessert.

The group of artists appear to have been great friends, the companionship being as important to them as the subjects and landscape. Many of the group became very well known and exhibited at the Royal Academy.

Forbes's painting of *A Fish Sale on a Cornish Beach*, painted in 1885, showed his great interpretation of light and atmosphere in his depiction of the fish on the sands. The success of this and many of his paintings brought fame to the Newlyn group as a whole, painting always out of doors in all weathers. Boats, quays, fishermen and their working wives – the paintings of all of the group are a wonderful record of Newlyn in the late nineteenth century.

Forbes married Elizabeth, a painter of some repute from Canada, whose first studio was a fisherman's loft where he mended his nets. She originally preferred the more exciting life of St Ives, but after marriage settled down in Newlyn with her husband and friends. She died in 1912, but Forbes went on to paint through the war years, until within a few years of his death in 1947 at the age of ninety.

While the railway opened up Cornwall as never before to visitors and artists, many of the inhabitants of Cornwall were leaving the county at this time, not by rail, but by sea.

The mines, which were flourishing at the beginning of the century, particularly the copper mines, were now suffering a decline. Other countries were producing copper, and there was a great emigration of out-of-work miners to America, Australia, South Africa and New Zealand, leaving as mementos the remains of the engine houses that are seen throughout Cornwall today.

A third of the mining population left Cornwall before the end of the century, taking with them not only their mining skills, but also their Methodism, their hymns and their skills in building their stonecottages and drystone walls. All this, together with their cherished possessions, they took to their new homes. Often they gave their new homes the name of the places they had left behind in Cornwall. Many of the Cornish surnames that have died out in Cornwall are found today in America. It was said that there was not a mine in the world at this time that did not have a Cornishman working in it.

Methodism had contributed greatly to the industrious qualities of these people. It had given them great spiritual fortitude to cope with both their material wants and their sufferings, whether at home or abroad.

Many had lived on small farms or in scattered groups. They were used to hardship and loneliness. Many even liked this comparative isolation, as had their Celtic ancestors, preferring to walk miles to work in a mine rather than live in a village. In spite of this they were willing to cross the Tamar for the first time in their lives, simply to go to an English port for embarkation to far lands. One woman from St Just, when asked if she had ever been to Land's End, six miles away, replied that St Just people didn't travel much, only to South Africa.

There was mass emigration from the Caradon copper mine, north of Liskeard, which had once employed four thousand. Hundreds left St Austell, Helston and St Just in the 1860s. Many wives and children were left behind until the fathers made enough money for them to join them.

In the meantime every parish had to support its poor. At the beginning of the century, when the harvest failed, a parish had to provide corn and barley at reduced rates for the poor, a cost covered by an increase in the rates.

As had always been the case, families prospered and fell in times of trouble in the nineteenth century – this applied to wealthy and poor alike.

The Trevanion family had owned the medieval manor of Carhays since the fourteenth century, when a Trevanion married into the Arundell family. In the nineteenth century the Gothic revival had set in, due in part to the novels of Sir Walter Scott, which created a great interest in medieval architecture and highly carved furniture. This inspired the then owner, John Trevanion, to call on the architect John Nash, one of the finest exponents of the new styles, to design the battlemented and turreted castle that can be seen today, with its subsequent improvements. The romantic setting on the shores of Veryan Bay, four miles south-east of Tregoney, adds to the castle's impressiveness, and the gardens designed by one of the great Cornish gardeners, J.C. Williams, serve to enhance its beauty. They are full of plants, the seeds for which came from Asia and which were developed to produce the wonderful variety of rhododendrons, camellias, magnolias and azaleas that flourish at Carhays today, thriving in the moist, acid soils that make such gardens a joy for visitors to this part of Cornwall. Unfortunately the great cost of this castle and its gardens ruined the Trevanion family, and after living at Carhays for twelve generations, they were forced to sell the estate in 1852 to the Williams family, one of the great families whose wealth had come from the Cornish mines, and who own the castle today.

This great burden of debt demoralized the family that had played such a prominent part in the history of Cornwall as knights and squires, serving the county in war and peace. Sir William Trevanion was an eminent member of the family at the time of the Wars of the Roses. When he died he left his wife his silver ewer and basin, his second-best salt cellar of silver with a cover, six silver spoons, a goblet of silver gilt, two bowls, a chalice, his best pair of vestments, altar cloths and silk curtains, and a Mass book for a chapel. His son was given the best feather bed, with its coverlet, bolster and sheets, but only his second-best horse, as the Dean of King's Chapel 'must have the best, of duty' (and presumably the best salt cellar).

By the middle of the nineteenth century, when the family had sunk so low in debt, the owner of Carhays was reduced to amusing himself by shooting the eyes out of the portraits of his family with pistols. The castle is now privately owned and cared for by the Williams family.

The Robartes family met their trouble when a fire destroyed Lanhydrock House in 1881. It was a disaster at the time, but was to leave us the wonderful legacy of a large Victorian family home when it was rebuilt. Using only local materials and craftsmen in the rebuilding, it gives a complete picture of the craftsmanship of Cornwall in its carving, panelling and plasterwork, as well as a picture of the life of the family who lived there until the middle of the twentieth century.

Not only was the house almost destroyed by the fire, which started, as so often was the case, in the kitchen chimney, but it also resulted in the death of the owners. Lady Robartes, at the age of sixty-eight, had to be rescued by ladder from an upstairs window, the shock being such that she died a few days later. Lord Robartes died the following year, undermined by the loss of both his wife and his home. Their son succeeded to the title and lived at Lanhydrock for the next forty-eight years. He rebuilt the house to be what was then thought to be a modest family home for his nine children. It was built to be fireproof as far as possible, with iron girders instead of wood, concrete floors and ceilings of a patent fireproof composition. Water, which had been in short supply at the time of the fire, was brought three miles through cast-iron pipes to a reservoir built on top of the hill above the house and conducted by hydrants to the building below. A boiler house below ground supplied a hot-water system as well as a central heating system, something not seen in England since Roman times.

There was a large painted cast-iron bath with a mahogany surround for Lady Robartes in the bathroom, the sides so high that a stool was needed to help her climb in. Her husband preferred to use a saucer-shaped bath in front of the fireplace in his own bedroom until his death in 1930. As originally rebuilt in 1883, that house had only one family bathroom, with a second for the nurseries.

For most homes toilet facilities did not improve until the end of the century. Water closets were installed in some houses, but they were not shown off as obvious home improvements. They were tucked away in a basement or in a yard at the back of the house. Chamber pots and commodes were the most usual toilet arrangements in a bedroom, usually heavily disguised, as is the one in the North Cornwall Museum, which when not in use masqueraded as a chest of drawers.

The usual washing arrangements in the bedroom were a marble-topped wash-stand with basin, jug and soap dish in a matching china set, and a can of hot water carried upstairs by the maid in the early morning. All the household were up early, servants and family attending morning prayers with a reading from the family Bible before breakfast. After this the whole of Lanhydrock must have been a hive of activity. All the servants would have been busy from the early hours lighting fires, cleaning grates, floors and carpets which were now more common. By the beginning of the next century they might have been lucky enough to have one of the first vacuum cleaners, although these sometimes required two women to work them. Inventions and engineering feats, active in industry in the nineteenth century, were slow to make life easier in the home. Servants to do the work were readily available. Nursemaids were also plentiful, and a large family of any position kept the children in their own nursery world, visiting or being visited by them at set times of the day. Families were large and mothers were kept in bed after the birth of a baby for anything up to a month. As a mother was more than likely to be in the same condition the next year, she probably needed this time to recover. Queen Victoria did mothers a great service when she gratefully accepted the use of chloroform at the birth of her eighth child, although she was much criticized at the time for doing so. After that it was widely used for the relief of those who could afford it.

In large households roasting was still done on spits, but in the Lanhydrock kitchen there was one alcove, where formerly there had been an open fireplace, now occupied by a closed-top kitchen range of cast iron, on the lines of today's solid-fuel cookers. Such ranges were in common use by 1860, even in small kitchens. There was a fire in the middle of the range, an oven on one side and hot-water boiler on the other, but this still had to be filled by hand.

The scullery at Lanhydrock had a small range where the stock-pot stood. The vegetables were prepared in the slate-lined sinks, where the kitchen pottery and utensils were also washed. All the ranges and fire grates in the house had to be black-leaded and the brass fire-irons, pokers, tongs, shovels and fenders all needed constant polishing.

The large kitchen was now within a reasonable distance of the dining room, which had a serving room next to it with a hot cupboard, heated by hot-water pipes, where the food could be kept warm after it was passed through a hatchway from the kitchen quarters.

Lady Robartes was able to deal with household matters from her sitting room next to the servants' quarters. At least these rooms were on the ground floor. In many nineteenth-century houses of any size in town and country, it was usual for the servants to work in the basement and sleep in the attics.

For so large a household (and at Lanhydrock the servants' quarters are larger than the family's), there was a bakehouse with a large bread oven which provided all the bread, scones, cakes and biscuits required. The oven had a proving oven below where the kneaded dough was put to rise. This oven and all the fires used coal by the truckload, which probably caused no problem in the country, although in towns the large amounts of coal consumed led to the fogs of which Charles Dickens left such vivid descriptions in his novels. The prevalence of coal-burning meant that spring cleaning became a necessity in Victorian times.

A passage from the bakehouse led to various larders for the preparation and storage of food – the meat larder, the fish larder and the dry larder, where the chef stored all the dry ingredients needed in his cooking.

The dairy, with an elaborate cooling system, was used for the storage of the jellies, blancmanges and elaborate cold puddings of the period, as well as soups, junkets and nursery puddings, and the cream, butter-milk and butter that had been prepared in the dairy scullery next to it. The latter room was one of the busiest in the house, with milk delivered to it from the estate farms twice a day. The dairymaids made large quantities of butter and prepared Cornish cream on a special scalding range heated by hot-water pipes.

The pantry and strong-room were in the butler's quarters. The strong-room contained the silver safe, guarded by the pantry boy who slept there each night. The butler's parlour and bedroom looked on to a little courtyard. Also in this male part of the house were the room of the steward of the estate and the smoking room and billiard room, well away from the family living rooms. Smoking was not approved of by Victorian ladies and required special clothes for the men and a special room where they could indulge in the habit – far removed from the family smoking round the fire in the seventeenth century. Billiard rooms became fashionable in any sizeable house in the nineteenth century.

While Lanhydrock had this multitude of rooms for every activity on a grand scale, many smaller homes were being built with extra rooms for their growing domestic needs. The prosperity of the middle classes in industrial areas enabled them to build large family houses, and many of the country people who had drifted in increasing numbers to the towns provided the servants necessary to run them. They were poorly paid but there was no shortage of them.

As the amount of clothing worn increased, with women striving to have 'a dozen of everything', particularly underwear, so the amount of laundry to be done increased. In small homes a separate wash-house was built to cope with the heat and steam, and a brick copper with a fire below to heat water and boil clothes. This wash-house became a warm place in which to take a bath, with hot water taken from the copper, the tin bath standing nearby. Large country houses had separate laundry rooms, unless the main wash was sent out to a local laundry or to someone in the village who ran a small laundry from her cottage.

Several irons of different shapes were heated on the range, including a small iron with a curved bottom to press the insides of sleeves or to use as a polishing iron to give a glazed finish to starched linen or chintz covers. Heavy Victorian suiting was pressed with a large, heavy iron known as a tailor's goose iron.

The first washing machine was a woman swirling the clothes about in a washing tub with a wooden 'dolly', the end of which was like a wooden stool. Only at the end of the century was a cast-iron clothes mangle introduced, with large wooden rollers, turned by a handle, between which the laundry was pressed.

Gas cookers at the beginning of the century were of cast iron, heavy and difficult to clean. Gas coppers achieved popularity more quickly, for heating water was a constant chore, as was carrying it. Most domestic work needed a strong right arm, as even when labour-saving devices were introduced they were at first usually worked by turning a handle. In the kitchen both floors and table-tops were scoured with sand. The stone floor of the scullery at Lanhydrock was cleaned with sawdust.

Given the ready supply of servants, the mistress of the smaller home found herself with little to do. For millions of Victorian women, the eighteenth-century promise of a fuller life outside their homes never materialized. Ironically, at a time when they were given so much more help in the home, the taboos of the age prevented them from taking advantage of this freedom.

That the Victorians were fond of their food is obvious. The kitchens at Lanhydrock are proof of this and required a large staff of servants, who also had to be fed themselves.

Food was, as it has always been, never far from the thoughts of the many visitors to Cornwall. One such was the Reverend Francis Kilvert, who left a careful record of his visit to Cornwall in July 1870. He travelled from Chippenham with a tourist ticket and was met by his friends, the Hockins, changing for Perranwell, then on by pony carriage to their home, Tullimaar. Getting around wasn't easy, but get around they certainly did during Kilvert's visit. Mrs Hockin drove him to Truro market along a road lively with market people – fine, tall people, especially the women, he noted, and most of them dark-haired. Mrs Hockin bought fish and poultry. There was a good variety of fish – red mullet, whiting, conger eels, turbot, John Dory and ray – on sale. But there were also boots, clothes and earthenware to be bought. They purchased Cornish pasties for their lunch. Then they sailed down to Malpas, bought a basketfull of ginger beer from an inn, and continued down to Falmouth Harbour, returning home by train.

Nothing daunted, they were up for breakfast at 6.45 the next morning and, travelling by pony carriage to Perranwell station, caught the 7.35 train to Hayle. Kilvert visited St Michael's Mount the same day.

At 9.30 the next day they were off to Mullion in a large wagonette that could carry ten people, drawn by a pair of greys. They ate their lunch at Gweek, at the side of a brook, while one of the horses was shod, having cast a shoe. Kilvert met a Mary Mundy, 'a genuine Cornish Celt', at the village inn. He said she was a good specimen, impulsive, warm-hearted, excitable, demonstrative, imaginative and eloquent. At the inn they went into an upstairs room, unpacked their hampers and ordered dinner to be ready in an hour's time, when they came back from visiting Kynance Cove. The next day was a visit to Falmouth Regatta, where Kilvert saw everyone dressed in their best clothes and gayest colours.

The following day they were off again on the 7.35 to Truro, which they caught with one minute to spare, travelling to Penzance, where they were met at the station by a small wagonette. In this they journeyed to Land's End, a trip punctuated by egg sandwiches and stops for sherry, ale and cider. They encountered parties of 'rude vulgar' tourists along the way, also vulgar picnic parties, forcing them to eat their dinner among the rocks, 'in aristocratic simplicity and seclusion'. After their walk to Land's End they met another 'noisy rabble of tourists'. There is no record of what the people they met thought of Kilvert and his party.

The next two days of his holiday were filled with expeditions and picnics. The only trouble was when going up one hill put a severe strain on the horses, causing a wheel to come off, nearly spilling the sherry. Dinner was at the Gurnards Mead Hotel and supper at midnight with friends at Camborne. Leaving at 1a.m. they arrived home about three in the morning. Kilvert's host lent him an Inverness cloak to protect him on the cold drive home on the top of the bus. This he had to return the next day, when after touring the area, they returned to their friends at Camborne for a meal of conger eel at eight and then back home for a hot supper of roast fowl at midnight.

Visitors did not find everywhere around the coast peaceful. The sea continued to take its toll of ships and men. The churchyard at Morwenstow contains relics of the many terrible wrecks that resulted from the storms on this dangerous north Cornwall coast. The vicar and poet the Reverend Robert Stephen Hawker, who lived and worked here from 1834 to 1875, gave Christian burials to those drowned sailors he was able to rescue with the help of his servants. They had to carry them some distance up the cliffs to the churchyard, where about forty of them are buried. The vicarage has chimneys representing the towers of the various churches where Hawker and his father were incumbents; the kitchen chimney represents his mother's tomb. On the cliffs nearby is the hut he built from the wood of shipwrecks. Here he wrote his poetry, much of it telling of the legends, shipwrecks and storms that had so occupied his life. The most famous of his poems, 'Song of the Western Men', has become a Cornish anthem. (See page 120)

Tennyson visited Hawker when he was touring Cornwall, absorbing more of the atmosphere of the county while working on his Arthurian poems. A great walker, he managed to walk ten miles a day in spite of 'furious rain'. He was often accompanied by Francis Turner Palgrave, whose *Golden Treasury* was dedicated to Tennyson. He wrote to the poet on 30 October 1860, 'Since I have returned I have worked steadily for two or three hours a day at making the collection of English Lyrical Poems we discussed in Cornwall', and added, 'Your encouragement, given while traversing the wild scenery of Treryn Dinas, led me to begin the work.' This cliff castle is on a spectacular headland near Treen, on the southernmost point of the Penwith peninsula.

We can wonder if Tennyson and Palgrave felt like the Reverend Kilvert did at the end of their visits: 'A bitter moment when the Tamar was crossed and Cornwall left behind, perhaps for ever. All the bright memories and names of the places (now so dear) together visited crowding up. The wild restless longing, the hopeless yearning, the gnawing hunger of regret.'

CHAPTER 11

The Once and Future Land

WHATEVER HAS OCCUPIED the Cornish Celts throughout their history, whether mining, religion or art, has all been undertaken against a background of hard-working farming and fishing. Everything has grown from these two activities, fundamental to the Cornish Celtic character. The land and the sea around it have developed the Celtic origins of the people and turned them into something unique. What they have become stems from the great influence nature in all its forms has always had on Celtic minds. The natural forces are so strong in Cornwall that they have affected everything the people have managed to achieve.

When the early saints set foot in Cornwall they must have found an environment that tested their faith to the limits as they struggled to feed themselves. How much they were helped by the farming communities that were already well established in the coastal areas we do not know. The lives of the early saints describe the hard work they were faced with in order to clear areas of woodland on which to grow their crops and build their homes and later their small monasteries. It was the same for the earliest Cornish farmers who had to clear bushes and undergrowth with axes. This process of clearance continued well into the Middle Ages.

The animals that were the most obvious sign of wealth to the Celts were also useful in consuming the new growth that appeared on the land after clearance, keeping it under control. Aerial photographs reveal Celtic fields that are still the same centuries later. The stones and granite boulders that had to be moved to enable the ground to be ploughed formed the boundary markers, and were not easily moved or destroyed.

Although chariots drawn by horses figure largely in Celtic stories, and there is evidence for these in other parts of Britain, there is not much sign of their use in Cornwall, although horses and carts as a means of transport of men and goods were no doubt an early part of Cornish life.

The early farming background of the Cornish revealed initially by archaeological evidence is emphasized in later years by manorial records and the records of the Duchy of Cornwall. The manors held under the old Earldom of Cornwall at the end of the twelfth century became the Duchy of Cornwall, created by Edward III in 1337. The history of the Cornish manors had been a turbulent one until the creation of the Duchy. They had passed back and forth between the Crown and various owners until Edward endeavoured to bring some stability to the situation. But the manors were profitable to whoever owned them: there was income from ports and havens, wrecks and royal fisheries, from tin mined on their land, and advowsons of all churches, abbeys and priories.

The records show that the manors were run efficiently, but with a system of farming unfamiliar in the rest of England. For the most part there was no open field system or common pasture. There were individual holdings, each with its own farmhouse, divided by the high hedges still found in Cornwall, necessary to provide shelter for men and animals as well as to mark boundaries. This was continuation of the way in which the Celts had always preferred to live, in scattered hamlets, or in isolation on moorland. Even when towns developed in the later Middle Ages, they were largely peopled by merchants and fishermen, often by foreigners. Most people found the towns useful as market-places, but they were not attracted to live in them. The isolated farms employed few labourers, so extended villages were not needed to house them. Many towns grew up around the larger monasteries, Bodmin and Launceston. Other towns came into being because their locations enabled them to be both port and market-place. The towns became the principal sites for markets and fairs.

Farms were rebuilt again and again on the same spot. Many modern farms are believed to have foundations that go back through the Middle Ages to early Celtic times. The fields adjoining these farms are rectangles or squares, about a half to one and a half acres in size, and can still be clearly seen on aerial photographs.

In the sixteenth century Richard Carew wrote that, after preparing the land, a farmer could raise two crops of wheat and two of oats. The land was then left fallow for at least seven or eight years. In the late spring pasture was cut up into turves which were dried and then burnt. The ashes were spread over the ground before they were ploughed in as potash. Sea sand was also used on the land. It was necessary to counteract the acidity of the Cornish soil and the sea sand was rich in lime. The farmers had the right to take what they required.

The mild Cornish winters allowed cattle to be kept out in the fields for most of the year. The corn produced was ground on hand querns until Norman times. At the time of Domesday, Cornwall had only six water mills for grinding corn.

The Black Death in 1348 changed much of the farming scene in Cornwall. It reduced the number of miners available to work in the tin mines, and labourers to work on the land were also in short supply. Many farmers increased the number of sheep on their holdings at this time. Sheep had always been numerous in the county but from the fourteenth century onwards their numbers increased and the textile industry expanded, and windmills and fulling mills appeared in the countryside.

Fulling mills were known in Cornwall as tucking mills. This was where the homespun cloth was dipped, cleansed and dressed. The tucking mills were in private ownership and were set up with the landlords' consent. Many cottages still bear the name of Tucking Mill, showing their earlier connections, before textile factories were established in the eighteenth century and took over this work.

Much of the land was held under lease from the duchy or was freehold, the latter being the most usual tenure. Mills, mill-ponds, ferries and fisheries were held in freehold. Services under duchy tenancies were mostly in connection with specific holdings, such as deer parks, or the maintenance of weirs. Some tenants paid for their tenancy with sheep.

The duchy leased land and buildings to many cottage-dwellers described as 'tuckers' and 'weavers'. Cornwall was acting as a supplier of yarn to the large clothing manufacturers in Devon in the sixteenth and seventeenth centuries.

In the parish of Sennan in the nineteenth century there were people known by the nickname 'Triddles', as their ancestors had worked the treadles while weaving at their looms. The textile industry later became organized by spinning masters and yarn jobbers, to the financial disadvantage of the spinners and weavers working in their cottages. The women around the fishing villages used the wool to knit many of the clothing items for their fishermen – jerseys, socks and hats.

The fishing industry mirrored the development of various aspects of agriculture. These two basic occupations were as intertwined as the patterns in Celtic art. The fourteenth and fifteenth centuries saw the expansion of fishing villages around the Cornish coast. Fishing had provided plentiful food from the earliest Celtic times, but soon the villages of Mevagissey, New Quay and Bude came to be mentioned for the first time in records. Small natural harbours acquired quays and breakwaters to create bays that would enable larger vessels to enter. This in turn provided an outlet for increased agricultural production to feed the growing population of these villages, whose people were engaged in activities connected with building and victualling ships coming to the ports.

When the fishing industry was at its height, the whole population of a village would be involved with boat-building, making ropes, nets, sails and hogsheads, the large casks used for transporting pilchards. The pilchard industry was particularly important to the villages and ports in the seventeenth and eighteenth centuries.

The picturesque villages that are so fascinating to visitors today grew out of the need of the increasing population to build homes, which were perched precariously on the limited land available, on the sides of hills leading down to rivers, estuaries and harbours.

The new harbours facilitated ships carrying stone from Cornish quarries and slate from Delabole, as well as the growing number of textile products. Fish was sent to London, Bristol, Southampton and Exeter, as well as to the Mediterranean, as it had been in the past. Ships brought wine and many new products back to Cornwall, as well as coal and wood to fuel the expansion of the mining industry.

St Michael's Mount had been a harbour and trading port from very early times, but in 1427 William Moreton petitioned the King for permission to construct a new harbour, which needed further improvement by Sir John St Aubyn in 1727, when the export of Cornish tin was at its height. This enabled Norwegian vessels to sail into the harbour

The Huer's hut at Newquay, restored in 1835. It has a large medieval chimney

with much-needed timber for buildings, boats and mines.

A new pier was constructed at St Ives at this time to cope with the expansion in fishing and enable larger merchant vessels to come to the town, which had grown from the small fishing village of its earlier days. The new pier needed a lengthy extension by the next century.

Many of the boats used in the industry were built in Cornwall, including the seine boats with their large nets which were forever in competition with those using draft nets.

The quantity of pilchards around the Cornish coasts at this time is hard to envisage today. When the huers, whose job it was to watch the sea, saw signs of the arrival of the fish, the cries of 'Heva, heva' resounded all round the coasts. This was a moment not to be missed. The entire population rushed to the shore to deal with the catch. A huer's hut still stands on the headland at Newquay where watch was kept. The fish were cured and stored in fish cellars around the coast. At the entrance to the cellars at Harlyn Bay is the inscription *'Dulcis lucri odor'* ('Profit smells sweet'), and for many hundreds of years so it did for Cornish fishermen.

The pilchards were stacked between layers of salt, or in a later method left in tanks of salt for several weeks. The salt was reused if it was still in a satisfactory condition. So much salt was needed in the eighteenth century that it had to be imported from France. In 1764, 800 bushels were sent to Mousehole and 1800 bushels to Newlyn. The oil that was pressed from the pilchards while processing them was used for lighting lamps, not only in Cornwall but also in London. Dealing with the fish after it was landed was mostly the work of women and children.

The locals brought their baskets and bussas, large pottery containers, to take home their own supply of fish to salt down for the winter, and this, with potatoes, constituted their main diet. Bussas were made at a pottery on Chapel Hill, overlooking the city of Truro and its cathedral. Originally the pottery used clay from nearby fields, but from the end of the seventeenth century most of the clay was brought from the north coast (where it was used by the local tinminers to stick candles on their hats and was known as 'candle clay'). The furze originally used to heat the kilns at the pottery was cut on Potter's Down on the outskirts of Truro, or purchased from professional furze-cutters, who brought it to the pottery in wagonloads to be stacked in ricks. About five hundred faggots of furze were used at a firing. Later, coal-fired kilns were used

Landing fish at Newlyn in 1880's

until replaced by gas and electric kilns. Workers from the Truro pottery would race with their wagons to the coast to sell their bussas when a glut of fish was reported. According to tradition,which claimed that their competitors' horses stopped at every public house on the way from force of habit, Truro pottery's wagon always won. But everybody made for the shore by whatever means possible, many coming from some distance in little donkey carts to collect the treasure from the sea.

Some of the pilchards were baked in a pie called 'Starry-Gazey Pie', which left the heads poking through the pastry, gazing at the stars. At Mousehole the pie is eaten every 23 December in memory of Tom Bowcock, who is honoured for saving the inhabitants from starvation two hundred years ago. Bad weather had prevented the inhabitants from putting to sea. Tom ventured out alone in great danger to search for fish, which he brought back to Mousehole, enough to feed every-body over that Christmas. Such was the importance of fish to the com-munity that he is remembered still.

The one monarch who really seems to have appreciated the fisher-men of Cornwall was Elizabeth I. She encouraged the eating of fish on 153 fast days, when meat was forbidden, long after the Reformation made it no longer obligatory to do so. She fully understood that these were the men who would be ready to man her ships to defend England when needed.

Fish was also on sale at the many markets in towns and villages, as the Reverend Kilvert discovered in Truro. The weekly markets were the most important centres for the distribution of food before the advent of shops. Much of it was dairy produce sold by the farmers' wives, and meat and poultry produced by their husbands.

The markets were great meeting places for the people of the sur-rounding countryside. The local inns provided food and drink in large quantities, which turned market days into festivals for the whole family. The markets were also the places where families could purchase boots and clothing. At the beginning of the nineteenth century there were thirty or forty stalls selling boots, some with two hundred pairs to a stall, in the market at Penzance.

The Celtic love of feasting is recorded in the very earliest stories. Today, when feeding the thousands of visitors to the county is of paramount importance, supplying plenty of food and drink is again occupying the inhabitants. It is something the people do well, from simple Cornish pasties and cream teas to gourmet meals of the highest standards in restaurants and hotels.

But it is not only the visitors who are fed. Feasting on parish saints' days, at village fairs, fêtes, chapel teas, harvest festivals, May Day festivities, to say nothing of family Christmases, keeps the provision of food high on the list of Cornish activities, and would gladden the heart of many an ancient Celt.

The Celtic spirit of the country is as strong today as it ever was. Strangely, it seems particularly vibrant in the extreme south-westerly part of the Penwith peninsula, where it was unaffected by outside forces and events for a longer period of time.

The stone circles and monuments here seem now to be acting as a magnet to those who visit them in their quiet settings. Perhaps without the distractions of the religious or magical ceremonies that took place here in antiquity, the sites have returned to the peace of their prehistoric beginnings. Maybe the rocks that once echoed to the clanging of the tin mines and the stamping of machinery are themselves rejoicing in the peace that now attracts visitors seeking the solace of these remote places, a solace often as difficult to find as the sites themselves.

The streams and rivers are content as always to flow gently through the Cornish woodlands, their spirits refreshing all who wander near them. Only the sea is unchanged, thundering against the rocks and cliffs one minute, calm and shining the next, and still the greatest influence on the Cornish people.

Now the younger generation of Celts have learnt to ride the waves on their surfboards with ever-increasing courage and skill. Many young people in Cornwall, both visitors and those who live and work there, find their inspiration and renew their spirits by challenging the waves, however wild they become. The Cornish beaches on the north coast in particular are so well known to the surfing community throughout the world that many important surfing events are held there.

Cornwall has adjusted to and accepted all the changes the twentieth century has brought. Not only only have the tourists been attracted to the county in their thousands, bringing mixed blessings, but there has been an unprecedented revival in one of the strongest aspects of Celtic life – the art and creativity of its people. While these may have been suppressed through the years of religious strife, war and industrial effort, all of which the Cornish pursued with the vigour of their ancestors, it now seems that the county again has time for the pleasanter side of Celtic life – the hospitality, art, music, literature, pottery and sculpture that have always been important to the Celts, and which charm all who come to Cornwall.

The influx of artists that started at the end of the nineteenth century continued unabated in the twentieth. The fishermen's cottages and fish lofts of St Ives, which were needed when the pilchard industry was at the height of its boom, were converted to artists' studios when the industry declined. Today there are many artists working in St Ives, both professional and amateur. There are numerous galleries where their work can be seen.

Making the most of redundant building, the St Ives Society of Artists, which was formed in 1927, is now situated in the Old Mariners' Chapel, built in 1905. This was originally built as a place of worship for fishermen, but fell into disuse as most of the population were Methodists who preferred their own simple chapels to large and imposing buildings. Members of the Society, which includes artists of established reputation as well as young painters and sculptors, hold regular exhibitions of their work there.

The old gasworks site overlooking Porthmeor beach was bought by the county council with the object of building a new Tate Gallery. Many St Ives artists already had their work on display in the Tate Gallery in London, of which the new gallery was to be a satellite, as is the Tate Gallery in Liverpool. Its object was to focus on the way art relates to a particular region, and also to show how the development of this art has been influenced by archaeology and natural and industrial history – very Celtic aspects of Cornish life.

The design of the gallery illustrates this very well. It enables visitors not only to enjoy the displays but also to look out on to the dramatic landscape of sea and harbour, and to Godrevy Island across St Ives Bay.

Designs were submitted by five architects, the final choice being Evans and Shalev, a leading firm with strong St Ives associations. They had won an award for their design of the new Courts of Justice in Truro.

The St Ives Tate Action Group was formed in 1990 and set about raising money for the building. Local artists held exhibitions of their work to this end, selling their paintings and opening their studios to the public. Writers joined in as well with a special Writers' Day, attended also by publishers, booksellers, poets and book collectors. The gallery was officially opened by Prince Charles, Duke of Cornwall, in June 1993.

It is not surprising that such a picturesque spot has attracted so many artists, but it is not only painters who are at work in Cornwall today. The ancient rocks and formations of the west have drawn potters and sculptors as well, among them some of the most famous in the world.

Pottery, which tells us so much about the ancient people of Cornwall, will no doubt enable the many potters at work there today to tell future generations their story. The greatest name in pottery in St Ives is that of Bernard Leach. He founded his pottery there in the 1920s and is one of the greatest influences in twentieth-century ceramic history. He was born in Hong Kong in 1887 and lived there until at the age of ten he came with his parents to England. After studying drawing at the Slade School, he returned to Japan in 1909 as an etcher. Eventually he met a younger man there, Shoji Hamada, who returned with him to England, where they set up the pottery at St Ives in 1920. The work begun there eventually made both potters world famous. Leach wrote *A Potter's Book*, first published in 1940, one of the most important books on pottery of this century. This was one of the many volumes he wrote inducing potters to work in a new way. He stressed the essential harmony of proportion, and both the practical and philosophical background to pottery. He passed on his experience and knowledge to potters everywhere, including his own family, several of whom are well known in their own right, including his son David and his grandson John, who is still busy at his pottery in Somerset.

Bernard Leach married another eminent potter, Janet Leach, who after his death in 1979 continued working in the pottery at St Ives and still works there today. She was an American who became interested in the philosophy and techniques of Japanese pottery after meeting Bernard and Shoji Hamada when they were on an American tour. She

Sculpture in Barbara Hepworth's garden museum at St. Ives

studied and worked in Japan, rare for a foreign woman. Her pottery is found in collections all over the world.

Barbara Hepworth, one of the great sculptors of the twentieth century, took her inspiration from the shapes of the rocks and trees around her, as can be seen today in the home in St Ives where she lived and worked. Visitors can walk among her works in her garden, which she left in her will as a permanent exhibition of her work. Some are small pieces, some massive, such as the 'Conversation with Magic Stones', carved in 1973. She was married in 1934 to Ben Nicholson, the painter, one of a group of artists with strong European influences. When war came many artists moved to America, but Hepworth and Nicholson moved to St Ives. Both were affected by the move to Cornwall and it brought changes to their work. Barbara Hepworth carved in wood and stone, observing the landscape and making it part of her carvings and the carvings part of the landscape. She emulated in her work the mysterious holes in the ancient stones, such as the one at Mên-an-Tol. Such works are shown to great advantage in her garden, letting in light and colour. Perhaps she understood the ancient stones better than we do.

Her sculptures travelled all over the world to exhibitions. She was one of the Cornish artists to be part of the Festival of Britain in 1951, together with some of the best-known Cornish painters – Peter Lanyon, Patrick Heron, Ben Nicholson, John Tunnard and Bryan Wynter. Musicians also featured, along with the Cornish-born composer and conductor, Michael Tippett.

Barbara Hepworth, Ben Nicholson and Bernard Leach were granted the freedom of the Borough of St Ives in 1968 in recognition of their international contribution to the arts. Hepworth had bought Trewyn Studio and gardens in 1949 and lived there until her death in a fire at her studio in 1972. The workshop is as she left it and the house is a museum dedicated to her work. She was created CBE in the New Year's honours list of 1958.

Dame Barbara Hepworth carved the Madonna and Child for the Parish church of St Ives, as well as designing the Christmas rose candlesticks on the altar. The statue was dedicated by the Bishop of Truro to her son, who was killed in a flying accident in Thailand while serving with the RAF. Altar candlesticks and a flower pedestal in the Lady Chapel were given by the sculptor Paul Mount. The floor tiles in the Island Chapel of St Nicholas are by Bernard Leach.

The art colony of St Ives grew quickly after the war. Hepworth and Nicholson exhibited at the St Ives Society's gallery, along with more and more artists working in both traditional styles and with modern and abstract ideas. Exhibitions from the Society toured the country. It seems it was not possible for artists to be unaffected by the county in their work methods and the variety of ways in which they viewed their surroundings. The inspiration that had affected the painters of Newlyn and St Ives in the last century still works for those of the present, wherever they settle in Cornwall.

Many of the Cornish artists have combined talents – they are sculptors and writers as well as painters. Such was Sven Berlin, one of the many writers who seem to have been especially drawn to Zennor and the moors above it. This very ancient area of quoits, circles and burial mounds has attracted many writers to live and work there, perhaps enticed by the legend of the mermaid of Zennor. She is portrayed in the very old carving on a bench-end in the church there. It is said that she heard a young man, Matthew Trewhella, singing in a strong tenor voice in the church every Sunday. She appeared to him as a beautiful lady, but always disappeared before the end of the service. One Sunday Matthew was able to follow her along a stream to the sea. He was never seen again, but a mermaid appeared to the captain of a ship, anchored off the cove years later, asking him to move and to stop blocking the entrance to her cave, where Matthew and their children were waiting for her.

D. H. Lawrence lived with his German-born wife at Zennor during the Great War, but ran into trouble with the military authorities on suspicion of being a spy. He was thought to be signalling to enemy ships and was eventually forced to leave Cornwall, with many regrets. He wrote about the Zennor landscape in his book *Kangaroo*.

Virginia Woolf and her husband lived at the end of the war in the same cottage that Lawrence had occupied. Her father had a house at St Ives, which she loved as a child. She described Zennor as one of the most beautiful places in the world, and loved its isolation. The poet John Heath-Stubbs wrote a poem to the mermaid at Zennor, which he described as at 'the end of time'.

The writers who stayed for even short periods in St Ives and district produced novels and poems inspired by the area. They are as numerous as the painters. Some lived in Cornwall. Sir Arthur Quiller-Couch, who wrote under the pseudonym 'Q', was born in Bodmin, and lived in Fowey, the area that so influenced Daphne du Maurier, who lived nearby. Many are well known today and are still writing, their fame spreading through the adaptation of their worked for television, sending a picture of Cornish life to a wider audience. The Poldark stories of Winston Graham have given pleasure to many when shown on TV. Some writers tell of the magic of Cornwall, some of the romance, some, such as W. H. Hudson, of the wildness and power of the landscape, while John Betjeman put his great love of Cornwall into his poems.

North Cornwall, which Betjeman loved, features in Charles Kingsley's novel *Westward Ho!*, which mentions the Grenvilles of Stowe. R. M. Ballantyne, the author of *Coral Island*, lived in Penzance and wrote of the Cornish mines. Thomas Hardy featured Cornwall in several of his stories, having met his first wife Emma near Boscastle. Then there was Compton Mackenzie living at Hayle and Howard Spring at Falmouth. E. V. Thompson, active today, won a Best Historical Novel award in 1977 with *Chase the Wind* and followed it with novels with both mining and fishing as their background. Another whose work has transferred to the TV screen is W. J. Burley of Newquay with his stories featuring the detective Wycliffe.

The writers who have been inspired to write by living in or visiting Cornwall are without number, as are the artists, illustrating that there must be a magical Celtic spirit at work in the county which cannot be accounted for just by the climate or the scenery. It is the spirit out which legends grow – the Celtic spirit. It is as if the storytellers of the past are still in Cornwall today, but unlike their ancestors they can write down the stories they tell for all to enjoy, not just a few listeners round a homestead fire.

This spirit also makes music, drawing musicians to the county. As well as festivals there are seminars both for young musicians and for those well established in the musical world. They come to Cornwall to recharge their batteries, as do so many visitors, who come to gaze, listen and absorb – what they may not know, but whatever it is it works, for they come year after year.

The independent Celtic spirit of the Cornish still emerges to protect their county when necessary. They are always fighting to preserve their fishing industry, which has ever growing problems of over-fishing in their coastal waters. The fishermen of Newlyn were quick to support their Canadian counterparts when fishing rights off Newfoundland were threatened in 1994. They understood their problems.

The Cornish are still fighting to preserve their countryside against excessive encroachment by caravans which threaten the very landscape that visitors come to see. Keeping the balance between necessary business development and protection of the environment is difficult, more so than in the past. The problems and dangers are different from those of days gone by, but the people still struggle to preserve the land that has served them well and provided for them for centuries. They can no longer be isolated as in the distant past, but they can work to keep the best of this past while adapting to changing conditions.

No doubt they occasionally wish that King Arthur would return to assist them in their quest, but in the meantime they work towards the future, in Celtic confidence.

Select Bibliography

Baring-Gould, S., *A Book of the West* (Methuen) 1902

Buckley, J. A., *The Cornish Mining Industry* (Tor Mark Press) 1992

Chadwick, Nora K., *Celtic Britain* (Thames & Hudson) 1963

Clark, Evelyn, *Cornish Fogous* (Methuen) 1961

Coate, M., *Cornwall in the Great Civil War* (Oxford) 1933

Dillon and Chadwick, *The Celtic Realms* (Weidenfeld & Nicolson) 1967

Digby, C. W., *Bernard Leach, Hamada and their circle* (Marston House) 1995

Ellis, Peter Berresford, *Celt and Saxon* (Constable) 1993

Elliott-Binns, L. E., *Medieval Cornwall* (Methuen) 1955

Fox, Aileen, *South West England* (Thames & Hudson) 1964

Fox, Caroline, *Stanhope Forbes and the Newlyn School* (David & Charles) 1993

Fiennes, Celia, *Through England on a Side Saddle* (Leadenhall Press) 1888

Green, Miranda, *Symbol and Image in Celtic and Religious Art* (Routledge) 1981

Halliday, F. E., *Richard Carew of Antony* (Andrew Melrose) 1953

Halliday, F. E., *A History of Cornwall* (Duckworth) 1959

Hatcher, John, *Rural Economy and Society in the Duchy of Cornwall 1300–1500* (C.U.P.) 1970

Hamilton, Jenkin A. K., *Cornwall and the Cornish* (Dent) 1933
Cornish Homes and Customs (Dent) 1934
Cornwall and its People (Dent) 1934

Henderson, Charles, *Essays in Cornish History* (Oxford Clarendon Press) 1935

Hodge, James, *Richard Trevithick* (Shire Publications) 1973

Hodgkin, L. V., *A Quaker Saint in Cornwall* (Longmans Green & Co. Ltd) 1927

Hoskins, W. G., *The Making of the English Landscape* (Hodder & Stoughton) 1955

Hubert, Henri, *The Rise of the Celts* (Constable) 1987

Lever, Tresham, *Godolphin His Life & Times* (Murray) 1952

Matthews, J. H. A., *History of the Parishes of St. Ives, Lelant, Towednack and Zennor* (Elliot Stock) 1892

Megaw, Ruth and Vincent, *Celtic Art* (Thames & Hudson) 1980

Pearse, Richard, *The Ports & Harbours of Cornwall* (Warne) 1963

Plomer, William, editor of, *Kilvert's Diary* (Cape) 1938

Powell, T. G. E., *The Celts* (Thames & Hudson) 1980

Rawe, D. R., *Cornish Villages* (Robert Hale) 1978

Ross, Anne, *Everyday Life of the Pagan Celts* (Batsford) 1970

ROWSE, A. L., *Sir Richard Grenville of the Revenge* (Cape) 1937
  West Country Stories (Macmillan) 1946
  The Cornish in America (Macmillan) 1969
  Tudor Cornwall (Macmillan) 1969

THOMAS, CHARLES, EDITOR, *Rural Settlement in Roman Britain* (Council for British Archaeology) 1966
  Britain and Ireland in Early Christian Times (Thames & Hudson) 1971
  Tintagel Papers (Institute of Cornish Studies) 1988

WEATHERHILL, CRAIG, *Cornovia* (Alison Hodge) 1985

WHYBROW, MARION, *Portrait of an Art Colony St Ives* 1883–1993 (Antique and Collector's Club) 1994

WRIGHT, MARY, *Cornish Treats* (Alison Hodge) 1986

The Journals of the Cornwall Archaeological Society

Index

Numbers in italics refer to
illustration captions

INDEX

Wales, Welsh, 26, 42–3, 44, 45, 46, 48, 50, 53, 60, 61, 74, 90, 125
Warbeck, Perkin, 91–2
Wars of the Roses, 64, 94, 142
Watt, James, 137
weapons and tools, 13, 15, 17, 25, 66, 67, 68
Wedgwood, Josiah, 132
wells, holy, 44
Wesley, Charles, 133, 135
Wesley, John, 133, *134*, 135–6
Whitesand Bay, 91
William I the Conqueror, King, 75, 77
William of Malmesbury, 61; *Deeds of the King of the English*, 61
William of Worcester, 46

Wiliams, J.C., 142
Williams family, 142, 143
Winslade, John, 99, 100
women, Celtic, 29, 37; graves of, 28, 68, *69*
Woolf, Virginia, 162
wrecks, wrecking, 93, 133, 148–9, 151
writers in Cornwall, 162–3
Wynter, Bryan, 161

Ygerne, 61
Youlton, bronze bowl from, 68–9, *70*

Zennor, 162; legend of the mermaid of, 162
Zennor Quoit, 16